CURRENT ISSUES BIBLE STUDY SERIES

Politics

D1532377

CHRISTIANITYTODAY

INTERNATIONAL

THOMAS NELSON

Since 1798

NASHVILLE   DALLAS   MEXICO CITY   RIO DE JANEIRO   BEIJING

Published in Nashville, Tennessee, by Thomas Nelson. Thomas Nelson is a registered trademark of Thomas Nelson, Inc.

Thomas Nelson, Inc. titles may be purchased in bulk for educational, business, fundraising, or sales promotional use. For information, please e-mail SpecialMarkets@ thomasnelson.com.

Editor: Kelli B. Trujillo
Development Editors: Kelli B. Trujillo and Roxanne Wieman
Associate Editor: JoHannah Reardon
Review Editor: David Neff
Page Designer: Robin Crosslin

ISBN 13: 978-1-4185-3426-4

Printed in the United States of America
08 09 10 11 12 RRD 6 5 4 3 2 1

CONTENTS

CONTRIBUTING WRITERS

Leith Anderson is pastor of Wooddale Church in Eden Prairie, Minnesota; he has also served as interim president of Denver Seminary and the National Association of Evangelicals.

Harold O. J. Brown serves as a professor of theology at Reformed Theological Seminary in Charlotte, North Carolina.

Stephen L. Carter is the William Nelson Cromwell Professor of Law at Yale University. He is the author of numerous books and is a regular columnist for *Christianity Today*.

Elesha Coffman is a graduate student in religion at Duke University. She was formerly the managing editor of *Christian History* magazine.

Charles Colson is founder of Prison Fellowship and was special counsel to President Richard Nixon.

Andy Crouch is editor of the Christian Vision Project (www.christianvision project.com)

Lee Eclov is senior pastor of Village Church of Lincolnshire, Illinois.

Timothy George is dean of Beeson Divinity School of Samford University and an executive editor of *Christianity Today*.

David P. Gushee is Graves Professor of Moral Philosophy at Union University and the author of several books.

Richard A. Kauffman is a former associate editor of *Christianity Today* and is now senior editor at *The Christian Century*.

Joy-Elizabeth Lawrence is a freelance writer living in Grand Rapids, Michigan, with her husband.

Brian McLaren is a pastor and author. He is a columnist for *Leadership Journal* and is involved in emergent, Call to Renewal/Sojourners, and other innovative Christian organizations.

Mark Moring is editor of ChristianityTodayMovies.com.

Nancy Pearcey is policy director of the Wilberforce Forum and executive editor of "Break Point," a daily radio commentary program featuring Charles Colson.

John Perry is a postdoctoral fellow at the University of Notre Dame.

James W. Skillen is president of the Center for Public Justice.

Alison Tarka is a stay-at-home mom, blogger, violinist, and freelance writer for small groups. She lives in Portland, Oregon.

Jason Tarka is a pastor in Portland, Oregon, where he leads worship, teaches theology, writes for small groups, and enjoys the best coffee in the country.

Kelli B. Trujillo is a writer, editor, and adult ministry leader at her church.

Bob Wenz coaches churches and trains pastors through Renewing Total Worship Ministries. He is a board mmember of the National Association of Evangelicals and an adjunct faculty member at Kings College and Seminary and at Pikes Peak College.

Betty Veldman Wieland worked for twenty-two years at Christian Reformed Home Missions (www.crhm.org). She co-authored with David Stark the book *Growing People Through Small Groups* (Bethany House).

William H. Willimon is Dean of the Chapel and professor of Christian Ministry at Duke University in Durham, North Carolina.

INTRODUCTION

Left? Right? or Center? Along with rifts over theological issues and worship practices, politics is a hot-button issue that often divides the church. For some, involvement in politics and with the state should be avoided at all costs; for others, political activism is a central avenue of expressing their faith. Some Christians view endorsement of one political party over another as a no-brainer; for others, the matter is much more complex. For some, political issues—such as the separation of church and state—are a source of great frustration; others view it as a source of great opportunity. Some view political involvement as a way to serve God and others; while other Christians view most politicians as corrupt, untrustworthy, and power-hungry. For some believers, the government is worthy of honor, respect, and trust; others are distrustful of the government and reject its claim of allegiance, determining to trust solely in God.

Discussing politics inevitably leads to differences of opinion; that's why many people avoid talking about it at all costs! But differences of opinion need not lead to division in your group; conversely, you can use this Bible study to get to know each other better, understand various approaches to theology and culture that may be different from your own; and most importantly, learn more from Scripture about what God says—and doesn't say—about politics. We hope this *Current Issues Bible Study* guide will help you grow closer as a group and challenge you in ways you may not expect.

For Small Groups

These studies are designed to be used in small groups—communities of people with a commitment to and connection with each other. Whether you're an existing small group or you're just planning to meet for the next eight weeks, this resource will help you deepen in your personal faith and grow closer with each other.

Along with the eight studies, you'll find a bonus Small-Group Builder article from Christianity Today's SmallGroups.Com. On SmallGroups. Com, you'll find everything you need to successfully run a small-groups ministry. The insightful free articles and theme-specific downloads provide expert training. The reproducible curriculum courses bring thought leaders from across the world into your group's discussion at a fraction of the price. And the revolutionary SmallGroupsConnect social network will help keep your group organized and connected 24/7.

Christianity Today Articles

Each study session begins with one or two thought-provoking articles from *Christianity Today* or one of its sister publications. These articles are meant to help you dive deeply into the topic and engage with a variety of thoughts and opinions. Be sure to read the articles before you arrive to your small group meeting; the time you invest on the front end will greatly enrich your group's discussion. As you read, you may find the articles persuasive and agree heartily with their conclusions; other times you may disagree with the claims of an article, but that's great too. We want these articles to serve as a springboard for lively discussion, so differences in opinion are welcome. For more insightful articles from *Christianity Today* magazine, visit http://www.ctlibrary.com/ and subscribe now.

Timing

These studies are designed to be flexible, with plenty of discussion, activities, and prayer time to fill a full small group meeting. If you'd like, you can zero in on a few questions or teaching points and discuss them in greater depth, or you can aim to spend a few minutes on each question of a given session. Be sure to manage your time so that you're able to spend time on the "Going Forward" questions and prayer time at the end of each study.

Ground Rules

True spiritual growth happens in the context of a vibrant Christian community. To establish that type of community in your small group, we recommend a few *ground rules:*

- Guarantee confidentiality. Promise together that whatever is said in the context of your small group meeting is kept there. This sense of trust and safety will enable you to more honestly share your spiritual struggles.

- Participate—with balance. We all have different personalities. Some of us like to talk . . . a lot. Others of us prefer to be quiet. But for this study to truly benefit your group, everyone needs to participate. Make it a personal goal to answer (aloud) at least half of the discussion questions in a given session. This will allow space for others to talk (lest you dominate discussion too much) but will also guarantee your own contribution is made to the discussion (from which other group members will benefit).

- Be an attentive listener—to each other and to God. As you read Scripture and discuss these important cultural issues, focus with care and love on the other members of your group. These questions are designed to be open-ended and to allow for a diversity of opinion. Be gracious toward others who express views that are different than your own. And even more important, prayerfully remain attentive to the presence of God speaking to and guiding your group through the Holy Spirit.

It is our prayer that this *Current Issues Bible Study* will change the lives of your group members as you seek to integrate your faith into the cultural issues you face everyday. May the Holy Spirit work in and through your group as you challenge and encourage each other in spiritual growth.

How should Christians

practice "right politics"?

SCRIPTURE FOCUS	
	Genesis 41:38–43
	Daniel 6:1–4
	Matthew 5:1–16, 38–48

DEFINING OUR
ROLE IN POLITICS

■

Who should you vote for? (Or should you vote at all?)

What party should you join? (Or should you even join in?)

How involved should Christians be in politics? (Or should we simply stay *out* of it altogether?)

Before addressing the issues you'll find in subsequent studies of this book (like differences between political parties, the separation of church and state, or America's identity as a "Christian nation"), we must first get our bearings by taking a look at the foundational question of whether politics should matter at all in the life of the Christian. In his *Christianity Today* article "Civic-Minded and Heavenly Good," James W. Skillen explores some important questions we may take for granted about the involvement of Christians in politics and civic institutions. Skillen deftly examines conflicting views about Christian identity and our role in society. Let's listen in on what he has to say and how the Bible informs the title question: How should Christians practice "right politics"?

■ Before You Meet

Read "Civic-Minded and Heavenly Good" by James W. Skillen from *Christianity Today* magazine.

CIVIC-MINDED AND HEAVENLY GOOD

How Christians should practice "right politics."

By James W. Skillen

"**P**rogress often comes from hurting others." That, according to Robert Kaplan, is Machiavelli's cruel but accurate assessment of political reality. And that is why America's political leaders today need a pagan rather than a Christian ethic if they are to defend American lives and interests. So says Kaplan, author of *Warrior Politics: Why Leadership Demands a Pagan Ethos* (Random House, 2002). "Machiavelli," says Kaplan, "believed that because Christianity glorified the meek, it allowed the world to be dominated by the wicked: he preferred a pagan ethic that elevated self-preservation over the Christian ethic of sacrifice."

Exactly right, says Duke University theologian Stanley Hauerwas. "War becomes the great event in American life, because that's when we send the young out to die and be killed. . . . It's an extraordinary sacrificial system, but sacrificing to the wrong god, Mars. . . . Christianity is an alternative to that sacrificial system" (quoted in Mark Oppenheimer, "For God, Not Country," *Lingua Franca*, September 2001).

Kaplan the political warrior and Hauerwas the pacifist agree: it is time to break up a Christian-pagan political marriage that should never have taken place. Kaplan thinks Christianity's private morality offers no public virtue. Hauerwas believes that Christianity's greatest virtue is displayed when Christ's followers renounce all use of violence. Furthermore, they say we can't have it both ways. If you want to protect America and the

---

best of its "private, Judeo-Christian morality," says Kaplan, you will have to work publicly to uphold good pagan virtue for "the preservation and augmentation of American power." On the other hand, if you want to be an undivided Christian, according to Hauerwas, you must relinquish the ungodly identification of Christianity with patriotism, and follow Christ, pure and simple.

Wrong and Right Politics

But are these the only two choices? Is there another way forward? Indeed, I believe the wholehearted following of Jesus Christ does entail a public ethos that stands in marked contrast to Kaplan's pagan ethos.

Furthermore, Christ's lordship sustains a role for human government that stands in marked contrast to the pacifism advocated by Hauerwas.

We need not dwell long on Kaplan's contention that Christianity offers no public ethic. His book is typical of those who are largely ignorant of Christianity and read it only through the eyes of Kant, Nietzsche, and Reinhold Niebuhr. Nietzsche, like Machiavelli, rejected as a grave human error the soft, unmanly meekness of Christianity. Niebuhr, though, is said to be the most important public theologian of the twentieth century. But his view of the direct public usefulness of the Christian love ethic was dim.

With Hauerwas, however, we must spend more time. First, he does not stand alone. He speaks for a growing community of Christians who look to the moral theology of John Howard Yoder and to the biblical exegesis of theologian Richard Hays. All three men believe that Jesus Christ has called his followers to live as an entirely new community—a new *polis* (Greek for "city"). The members of this polis worship, evangelize, and pursue social justice together as an alternative society that lives in contradiction to the world.

In an important 1979 essay titled "The Spirit of God and the Politics of Men" (published in *For the Nations*, Eerdmans, 1997), Yoder argues that Christians should,

> be guided by the claims of God upon the one real world which he intends by the power of his Spirit to redeem. The choice or the tension which the Bible is concerned with is not between politics and some-

thing else which is not politics, but between right politics and wrong politics. Not between "spirit" and something else which is not spiritual, but between true and false spirits. Not between God and something else unrelated to God, but between the true God and false gods.

Hauerwas fully affirms Yoder's call for a "right politics" of the Christian community. And that, Hauerwas insists, demands a politics of nonviolence. "That Christians are committed to nonviolence does not entail, as is often assumed, that Christians must withdraw from the world. The church of Jesus Christ must be in the world as he was in the world." Yoder's case for Christian nonviolence, says Hauerwas, "is compelling because his understanding and justification of nonviolence cannot be separated from the Christian conviction that God is our Creator and Redeemer. Yoder forces us to see that the doctrines of God and nonviolence are constitutive of one another" (*With the Grain of the Universe*, Brazos, 2001). Nonviolence is thus central to the church and "right politics." And this should be on display in God's new political community, the church.

To sum up, then, these authors believe Christians are called to live in an entirely new community, a new polis. And this polis should be characterized by, among other traits, nonviolence.

But are these ideas biblical?

Misuse of Violence

Let's begin with the issue of nonviolence. This is where New Testament scholar Richard Hays comes in support of Hauerwas and Yoder. Hays contends in *The Moral Vision of the New Testament* (HarperSanFrancisco, 1996) that Yoder and Hauerwas are correct. From Matthew to Revelation, writes Hays, "we find a consistent witness against violence and a calling to the community to follow the example of Jesus in accepting suffering rather than inflicting it."

Yet Hays handles the words violence and nonviolence in a way that obscures the scriptural texts he deals with. Violence, as Hays uses it, always denotes or connotes "inflicting suffering" on others, hurting or killing or forcefully taking advantage of others. Furthermore, *violence* is the word that all three authors use when referring to the actions of the military and police. Hays concludes that the New Testament teaches that violence can never be used in the defense of justice. Consequently, true Christian community can have no part in the political communities of this world. Instead it is an alternative polis, a different kind of city. It is a community with a government quite unlike that of the United States or any other country.

But Hays fails to take up the Bible's actual language about the use of force. The New Testament does not use the word violence to refer to all uses of force. It, like the Old Testament, speaks of reprehensible acts of murder and killing. It also speaks of vengeance, retribution, and punishment. It says the killing of one's neighbor is murder and merits punishment. Biblical writers do not portray the use of force to punish the murderer as a parallel evil, but as just retribution. The punishment of the murderer by a God-ordained government is just recompense, not unjust violence.

The argument turns on Romans 12 and 13. From Yoder's highly influential *The Politics of Jesus* (1972) up through Hays's *Moral Vision*, these three theologians interpret this passage as follows: God condemns all violence, including the taking of vengeance upon one's neighbor. Instead, Paul urges Christians to return good for evil and to leave wrath to God (12:17–21). Consequently, since the responsibility of government includes the use of force against evildoers (13:3, 5), governmental offices are off-limits to Christians. That kind of government is part of the politics of violence and cannot be part of the Christian polis, or political community.

Quite in contrast to this interpretation, another one flows much more naturally and coherently from the epistle. Indeed, Paul, like Jesus in the Sermon on the Mount, tells Christians that they should return good for evil and turn the other cheek. Their lives are to exhibit loving service to their neighbors. Personal vengeance is off-limits because it grows from pride and self-seeking. Leave revenge to God, says Paul, because, as the Scriptures say, "'Vengeance is mine; I will repay,' says the Lord" (12:19).

Yet it follows directly from this, according to Paul, that God has established governing authorities precisely in order to execute some of that divine vengeance (13:1, 4). Government bears this responsibility not as an extension of human vengeance but as a servant of God. Government is not the independently authorized power of Caesar, but "God's minister to you for good" (13:4).

This is in keeping with the Old Testament and with the whole tenor of his letter. Paul is telling Roman Christians to recognize Christ's lordship by loving and serving their neighbors for their good, in every office they may hold. They should do this by responding nonviolently personally to any attacks—and by allowing God, through the governing authorities, to execute any forceful judgment that may be necessary against those who do such evil things.

If Christians find themselves in positions of governing authority, they must recognize, as every official must, that they are servants of God's justice. They are not personal vengeance-takers or representatives of vengeful friends and neighbors. In a position of political authority, their task is still to do good to their neighbors. But in this office, that will require punishing evildoers as well as commending those who do good. It is no contradiction for a Christian, on the one hand, to exercise restraint by not taking personal vengeance, and on the other hand, to exercise the responsibilities of a God-ordained office by executing God's vengeance. In both cases one is called to act as a wholehearted, undivided servant of the Lord. And in both cases one must be willing to sacrifice one's life for the good of one's neighbors in carrying out that service.

Beyond Alternatives

But the issues raised by these three thinkers go deeper than the narrow question of the use of force. They extend to the very identity of "Christian community." The Christ presented to us by the Gospel writers and apostles is the one who announces upon his resurrection that "all authority has been given to me in heaven and on earth" (Matt. 28:18). He is the Lord before whom every knee will bow and every tongue confess (Phil. 2:10–11). He is the one for whom all thrones and powers, all rulers and authorities, were created (Col. 1:16). Clearly, Jesus did not call his disciples to engineer the fulfillment of his kingdom by force, or to compel anyone to bow before the risen Lord (Matt. 13:24–30, 36–43; Acts 1:6–8). Yet as these passages show, Christ's lordship extends beyond the community of believers. The Christ whom we have been called to serve is not only head of the church but also the supreme authority in everything in heaven and on Earth (Col. 1:17–20). The implications of this confession for our life in society are huge.

Just as marriage and family life belong by creation to people outside the household of faith, so business and agriculture, science and art, schooling and government belong to all human creatures. I agree entirely with Yoder that the Bible is concerned with the difference between "right politics and wrong politics." Christians should indeed be demonstrating faithfulness as a community by the way they pursue "right" families, "right" businesses, and "right" politics. However, in imagining that we should pursue right politics through the church as an alternative polis, Yoder, Hauerwas, and Hays confuse the Bible's teachings on creation and redemption.

The followers of Christ are certainly a called-out community, called out from sin to become a community of obedience to God. But they are not called out of God's creation. Think for a moment of the biblical language used to characterize Christ's followers: bride of Christ, the children of their Father in heaven, brothers and sisters of their elder brother Jesus, joint heirs with Christ, a community of priests, disciples (students) in the school of a new teacher, and certainly citizens in Christ's kingdom. The primary referents in all of these metaphors are the very creaturely realities in which the people of God live.

To live as a member of God's family, I do not disown my parents but rather obey them as unto the Lord. Likewise, in order to participate in the Christian community as a citizen of Christ's polis (kingdom), I do not take leave of my citizenship. Rather, I act as a citizen in obedience to the Lord in accord with teachings such as those in Romans 12 and 13. The church, then, is not an alternative to any of these creaturely realities. It represents, instead, the fulfillment of them all in Christ.

The three theologians confuse matters by speaking of the church as an alternative polis. They would equally confuse us if they spoke of the church as an alternative family, or as an alternative business enterprise, or as an alternative school. The church is not an alternative to anything that God created for human development. Rather, the Christian community is that people whom God has restored to their creaturely callings as forgiven sinners, who are being redeemed by their Savior, Jesus Christ. The Christian community is composed of those who are learning to turn from habits of sinful degradation in all areas of life and seeking to demonstrate God-honoring earthly stewardship. Only when Christ's kingdom comes in its fullness will God put the full "alternative" community on display. And of course at that point of eschatological celebration, the people of God will constitute the creation fulfilled.

Christians may pretend in this age to live in a community they call an alternative polis, which among other things renounces the use of force for the sake of justice. But calling such a community a "political community" will not make it so. And in the meantime, the Kaplans of this world will go on deciding, with a pagan ethic, how to use military and police force. They have concluded that Christianity has nothing to offer, no criteria for judging the just and unjust performance of governments.

Instead, to be authentic Christians, to be able to serve our civic neighbors throughout the world, Christians need to be involved as real citizens in real governments, exhibiting a genuinely Christian public ethic. Such a responsibility will include working for the restraint of personal vengeance. And it will entail the exercise of official, publicly accountable punishment of those who commit crimes and unjust aggression.

Turning from injustice, faithlessness, hatred, and greed in every sphere of life requires constructive, communal service by those who are being redeemed from sin. When Christ, by the power of the Spirit, has finished making all things new, we will then be able to sing with the saints of all ages, "The kingdoms of the world have become the kingdoms of our Lord and of his Christ, and he shall reign forever and ever" (Rev. 11:15).

James W. Skillen is president of the Center for Public Justice (www.cpjustice.org).

("Civic-Minded and Heavenly Good" was originally published in Christianity Today on November 18, 2002.)

■ Open Up

Select one of these activities to launch your discussion time.

Option 1

Discuss one of these icebreaker questions:

- Describe your personal involvement in politics. Have you ever ran for (or held) public office? Have you ever actively campaigned for someone? Do you usually vote? Or do you tend to avoid politics? Explain.

- Name a political leader you admire, either from history or from recent times. What stands out to you about that person?

- What do you see as the most important traits of a good political leader? Is Christian faith on your list of traits? If so, how important is it to you? If it's not, why not?

Option 2

Read the following statements and write whether you agree, partially agree, or disagree. When everyone has finished marking their answers, discuss the questions at the end of this section as a group.

1. It would be ideal to have a government populated by Christians whose political decisions would be strongly influenced by their faith in Jesus.

   ☐ Disagree ☐ Yes, but . . . ☐ Agree

2. Christians should not vote, serve in government, or work for the state in other roles. Our loyalty and allegiance is to Christ alone; Christians who work for the state ultimately find their loyalty divided as they take part in an inherently corrupt institution with values that are contrary to the teachings of Jesus.

   ☐ Disagree ☐ Yes, but . . . ☐ Agree

3. Christians should serve in government in order to bring about moral laws and just actions by the state. Though at times Christians involved in politics may have to compromise on some issues, this is a necessary cost for a greater good.

   ☐ Disagree ☐ Yes, but . . . ☐ Agree

4. A good political leader must be strong, proud, and willing to fight for the best interests of one's nation, even when such preservation requires morally questionable actions such as killing (in war) or causing starvation (through economic sanctions). A leader's job is *not* to love one's enemies. Practically speaking, a good leader should be someone who is unreligious or someone who is willing, when necessary, to put Christian teachings aside for the cause of the state.

   ☐ Disagree ☐ Yes, but . . . ☐ Agree

5. Christians should feel a moral obligation to vote, particularly when the issues at hand relate to matters of central importance in Scripture. Christians who choose to abstain from political involvement and do not vote are morally culpable for the results.

   ☐ Disagree   ☐ Yes, but . . .   ☐ Agree

6. Christians should be involved in politics, but only within certain limits. They should vote, obey laws, and generally be good citizens. But they should not actually serve in government roles because their first loyalty must be solely to God, not the state.

   ☐ Disagree   ☐ Yes, but . . .   ☐ Agree

7. Christians should be politically active by functioning as a "thorn in the side" of the government: actively protesting or purposefully resisting unjust or immoral policies. In this sense, Christian activists serve as the conscience for a corrupt political system.

   ☐ Disagree   ☐ Yes, but . . .   ☐ Agree

8. Christians should view involvement in civic life as a duty and should honor those who choose to serve in the military and government. Working for the state is a direct and practical avenue of loving one's neighbor. It gives Christians a platform to powerfully be "salt" and "light" in society.

   ☐ Disagree   ☐ Yes, but . . .   ☐ Agree

- Which of the statements above best reflects your own view on Christians and political involvement? Why?

- With which of the statements above do you most strongly disagree? Why?

■ The Issue

In his article, Skillen quotes John Howard Yoder as saying: "The choice or the tension which the Bible is concerned with is not between politics and something else which is not politics, but between right politics and wrong politics."

- What do you think Yoder means here? What do *you* see as "right politics" and "wrong politics"? What issues, tensions, or ideas come to mind for you?

Skillen agrees with those he critiques—Hauerwas, Yoder, and Hays—that the Christian stance in the world is not apolitical. Christians don't try to escape political responsibility by going off into the desert to live a separate existence.

However, Skillen takes exception to these three theologians who seem to agree that the way the Christian is to be political in the world is through the corporate life of the church that witnesses to the lordship of Christ overall; and that this church-shaped politic demands that Christians are committed to nonviolence under each and every circumstance.

On the one side of this argument are those who say that violence must never be used in the pursuit of justice—or at least that Christians shouldn't participate in such use of violence. On the other side are those, like Skillen, who believe that the use of violence is sanctioned by God's ordination of governing authorities in Romans 13.

- What do you think? At first glance, which of these viewpoints best matches your own? Explain.

- What do you see as the strengths and weaknesses of each viewpoint?

■ Reflect

Take a moment to read **Genesis 41:38–43, Daniel 6:1–4; Matthew 5:1–16, 38–48** on your own. Write a few notes and observations about the passages: What phrases or examples are most helpful to you in understanding these issues? How would you summarize the key ideas in these passages? What questions do these passages raise for you?

■ Let's Explore

As part of the Good News of the gospel, Jesus invites us into a community of his disciples who are a leavening influence in society.

Matthew 13:33 records this short parable: "Another parable He spoke to them: 'The Kingdom of heaven is like leaven, which a woman took and hid in three measures of meal till it was all leavened.'"

- How do you feel God wants Christians to work as "leaven" in our society? What are some examples you've observed of Christians having a leavening influence?

Read **Matthew 5:13–16**. As you do, imagine what it would have been like to be one of Jesus's first followers.

In Jesus's day the Romans controlled Israel. In this setting, there were numerous religious groups defined by their relationship to the Roman Empire. The Essenes were like the Amish of their day. They attempted to maintain religious purity by withdrawing from the dominant culture. The Sadducees, on the other hand, sold out to the ruling empire and served as its lackeys. The Zealots were the liberation theologians of their day, who wished to overthrow the Romans by force. The Pharisees made what adaptations were necessary in order to carve out the religious space they needed to maintain the ritual purity of their faith.

Jesus didn't cast his lot with any of these groups. His message was simple, though demanding: *repent* because the rule of God—not Caesar's rule—is at hand, *believe* the Good News (of salvation), *take* up your cross, and *follow* me. In other words, live not just with me but like me, even if it means suffering and death. Living for Jesus meant—and means—living with Jesus and with the circle of people who surrounded him—and still surround him—what we now call the church, but what in Jesus's day were simply Jesus's disciples.

This motley band of disciples he gathered didn't withdraw from society; they didn't try to control it or overthrow it; they didn't even try to "just fit in." Together—in their relationships with Jesus, with each other, and people outside this band—they served as light in darkness, salt, and a leavening influence in society. Jesus's community has sometimes been referred to as the "contrast society," which is different from saying it rejects the dominant culture. The rule that prevails in this community is love—what Paul called the "more excellent way" (1 Cor. 12:31b)—and servant-hood rather than people lording it over others (Matt. 20:24–27).

- How did Jesus's band of disciples act as a leavening agent in their society?

- How can a "contrast society" affect change? Have you seen this done by anyone in today's culture? Who?

God can mightily use his people in positions of leadership and influence, including positions in the government.

- What are some contemporary examples of Christians in positions of power who've been used by God to do good in the world? How about examples from history? Describe them.

The Old Testament contains several examples of godly leaders who governed God's people, particularly kings like David, Josiah, or Hezekiah. But these kings ruled in a type of quasi-theocracy, leading a nation in worshipping and serving God. The case can easily be made that governing then was *much* different than being involved in government now in our country. After all, our country, on the whole, does not serve and worship God. Further, there are many immoral laws and practices inherent in our governmental system.

But Scripture also contains accounts of godly men and women who played significant roles of influence in governing pagan nations, most notably Joseph (Genesis 41:33–57) and Daniel (Daniel 6:1–28).

Take another look at **Genesis 41:38–43** and **Daniel 6:1–4.**

Alongside Joseph and Daniel is the story of Queen Esther. Though governance wasn't her profession as it was for Joseph and Daniel, the Bible does record a significant time in which she intervened in legislative matters; God used Esther's position and courage to sway her husband's political decision and save many lives. (See Esther 4–9.)

- What does Scripture record about the way in which Joseph and Daniel did their jobs? How were they regarded by their superiors? (See especially Genesis 41:38–40 and Daniel 6:3.) What insights do their stories offer for Christians today and our civic or political involvement?

- Beyond evangelism or talking about matters of faith, how should a Christian in a position of power serve God through governance? What should distinguish that person's leadership and decision-making?

In his treatise *Ethics,* Dietrich Bonhoeffer wrote,

As a citizen the Christian does not cease to be a Christian, but he serves Christ in a different way. This in itself also provides an adequate definition of the contents of the authentic claim of the government. It can never lead the Christian against Christ; on the contrary, it helps him serve Christ in the world. The person who exercises government thus becomes for the Christian a servant of God.

According to Bonhoeffer, God seeks not only to use leaders, but also regular citizens; our own involvement in civic life and government can be an avenue of service to Christ.

- Do you agree with Bonhoeffer? Why or why not? What do you think it should look like for a Christian to distinguish himself as a "good citizen"?

We are also called to challenge the powers that be by holding fast to Jesus's revolutionary teachings.
Consider Matthew 5:1–16, 38–48.

- Which of the statements or ideas in this passage do you feel contrasts most sharply with the values of our current government? Explain.

Beyond his instruction that we "Render therefore to Caesar the things that are Caesar's, and to God the things that are God's" (Matthew 22:21), Jesus does not say much directly related to the issue of politics and governance. But some, such as John Howard Yoder, point to Jesus's teachings in Matthew 5 as directly related to politics in the sense that here Jesus gives his followers specific instructions for how we are to live and what values we are to uphold. This text is foundational to Yoder's thought-provoking book *The Politics of Jesus.*

Regardless of whether we hold to the views of Yoder and Hauerwas or tend more toward Skillen's line of thinking, it is clear that Jesus's teachings in Matthew 5 directly challenge the values and assumptions of those in power in the first century as well as those in power today. We followers of Jesus aren't merely to affirm these teachings as good ideas; we are to *live* by them—even Christ's most radical assertions. It is by living in this way that we shine as lights in the world.

At times, holding to the values Jesus outlined may lead us to abstain from political involvement, resist governmental policies, or participate in acts of civil disobedience.

Martin Luther King and other civil rights leaders serve as a poignant recent example of Christians holding firmly to Jesus's revolutionary teachings and challenging the powers that be.

- How do you see aspects of Matthew 5 reflected in America's civil rights movement? What are some other examples, from history or recent times, of Christians who actively challenged governmental policies because of their commitment to Jesus?

Jim Wallis, author of *God's Politics*, said this on the National Public Radio program *Speaking of Faith*:

God isn't a Republican or a Democrat, and faith shouldn't be in any parties' political pocket. We should be the ultimate swing vote, if you would, holding both sides accountable. . . . [S]omething prophetic is growing again around the country. And I think it's going to change the whole political landscape. Politics is failing to solve the big issues. When that happens, social movements rise up to change politics. And the best social movements always have spiritual foundations.

- What do you see as the main areas in which Christians should be speaking out prophetically in the arena of politics? In what areas should we hold the Democratic party accountable? The Republican party?

In his book *God's Name in Vain,* Stephen L. Carter remarks that "Politics needs morality, which means that politics needs religion. . . . [T]he religious voice, at its best, is perhaps the only remaining force that can call us to something higher and better than thinking constantly about our own selves, our own wants, our own rights."

- How do you feel God may want you to call the world "to something higher"? Do you feel challenged to do this through civic involvement, through active resistance, or through abstaining from the political arena? Explain.

■ Going Forward

Form pairs to discuss the next two questions.

In his article, Skillen asserts that, "To live as a member of God's family, I do not disown my parents but rather obey them as unto the Lord. Likewise, in order to participate in the Christian community as a citizen of Christ's polis (kingdom), I do not take leave of my [national] citizenship." He goes on to say, "Instead, to be authentic Christians, to be able to serve our civic neighbors throughout the world, Christians need to be involved as real citizens in real governments, exhibiting a genuinely Christian public ethic."

- Do you agree with Skillen? Why or why not?

- Describe what you see as a "genuinely Christian public ethic." With your partner, list up to ten issues or characteristics that you view as essential to a Christian's approach to politics.

Gather back together as a group and share your lists with each other. Talk about how you feel personally challenged to live out the values you've discussed. Then pray together about the issues and characteristics you discussed. Also, pray by name for Christians you know of who are in positions of political leadership.

■ Want to Explore More?

Recommended Resources

Want to explore this topic further? Here are some resources that will help.

Ethics, Dietrich Bonhoeffer (Touchstone, 1995; ISBN 068481501X)

For the Nations: Essays Evangelical and Public, John Howard Yoder (Wipf & Stock Publishers, 2002; ISBN 1592440843)

God's Name in Vain: The Wrongs and Rights of Religion in Politics, Stephen L. Carter (Basic Books, 2001; ISBN 1581732295)

The Moral Vision of the New Testament: Community, Cross, New Creation, A Contemporary Introduction to New Testament Ethics, Richard B. Hays (HarperOne, 1996; ISBN 006063796X)

Warrior Politics: Why Leadership Demands a Pagan Ethos, Robert D. Kaplan (Random House, 2001; ISBN 0375505636)

Should Christians' ballots

look the same?

SCRIPTURE FOCUS

Matthew 5:43–48

Ephesians 4:1–5

VOTING DIFFERENCES

■

You've seen how this works. A pastor, Christian leader, or layperson endorses a particular candidate publicly or privately. Word gets around and an outcry ensues. "How can you support this person? Look at the voting record here; he (or she) doesn't care about God's creation/the poor/unborn children/innocent war victims/ the Constitution/traditional families/the working class/the homeless/the unjustly imprisoned/domestic security/the First Amendment!" What happens then? Must Christians come to a particular agreement about politics? Does being Christian automatically mean that we are to vote for one particular candidate or follow one particular party? Is it OK to disagree? When we do disagree, how are we to do it? In the following articles, "What's Right About the Religious Right" by Charles Colson and "Faith and Politics After the Religious Right," an interview with Brian McLaren, we'll hear two different voices on the topic of Christian politics and explore new ways of responding to these consistently tricky issues.

■ Before You Meet

Read "What's Right About the Religious Right" by Charles Colson and "Faith and Politics After the Religious Right," an interview with Brian McLaren.

WHAT'S RIGHT ABOUT THE RELIGIOUS RIGHT

by Charles Colson

The debate on the relationship of Christians to the state is nothing new and must be seen in historical perspective. The early church wrestled with the question as it faced the pagan Roman Empire; the tension continued in the medieval struggles between pope and emperor and on into the era of nationalism and the "divine right" of kings.

In the twentieth century, the debate has produced wide swings among conservative Christians between the extremes of isolationism and political accommodationism. In the early decades, believers were buffeted by the winds of theological modernism (with its social gospel), humiliated by the Scopes trial, and finally retreated into fundamentalist enclaves to create a parallel culture through their churches and schools. (The words we hear today from Paul Weyrich are hauntingly reminiscent of that time.)

Then, in 1947, Carl Henry published *The Uneasy Conscience of Modern Fundamentalism* and led Christians back into the American mainstream. What really galvanized them, however, was the liberal victory in *Roe v. Wade*. In one swoop, the Court struck down abortion laws in all fifty states, turning around an entire culture on the most crucial moral issue of the day.

The lesson was not lost on moral conservatives: they concluded that top-down political action was the most effective means of cultural transformation. If liberals could do it, so could they.

Thus was born the so-called Religious Right, which did fall prey to some of the excesses Cal Thomas and Ed Dobson diagnose in *Blinded by Might*. Enormous effort went into raising funds and garnering votes—

often with extravagant promises to "save America" if we would just elect the right candidates and pass the right bills.

At the time I created consternation among my conservative friends by warning that the church stood in danger of succumbing to the political illusion and allowing the gospel to be taken hostage to a political agenda. Much of the political rhetoric smacked of triumphalism. "We were on our way to changing America," Thomas and Dobson write. "We had the power to right every wrong and cure every ill." In short, at its worst, the Religious Right was a mirror image of the secular Left.

But if the earlier hope to "save America" was overblown, so too is the current counsel to withdraw from politics—an overreaction against an original overreaction. In the elegant words of Richard Neuhaus, such pessimism "expresses a painful deflation of political expectations that can only be explained by a prior and thoroughly unwarranted inflation." Were Christians in fact to withdraw, we would simply ride a pendulum swing back to the isolationism of the fundamentalist era.

Instead, we should learn from our mistakes and develop a biblically grounded political philosophy that gets us off the pendulum and provides a basis for acting "Christianly" in politics. The classic elements of a Christian worldview—Creation, Fall, and Redemption—should guide our thinking.

The doctrine of Creation tells us the state is ordained by God; therefore, participation in political life is a moral obligation, contained in the cultural mandate to cultivate the world God created. We should seek justice and order in political structures, striving to be the best of citizens, as Augustine put it, because we do for love of God what others do only because they are coerced by law.

Yet, because the state is not the only social institution ordained by God, we must work to keep its scope limited. We cannot let it usurp the place of other institutions, such as church and family (Abraham Kuyper's "sphere sovereignty"). Nor should we confuse what can be achieved by political means with what can be achieved only by spiritual transformation.

Second, because of the Fall we must be realistic about the limits of political success. This side of heaven, our accomplishments will always be partial, temporary, and painfully inadequate. There is no room for triumphalism.

Yet, third, neither is there room for despair, for the promise of redemption is that even in a broken world there can be healing and restoration. All creation came from God's hand, all creation was affected by the Fall, and by the same token, all creation shares in Christ's redemption. Salvation is not about personal renewal alone, but also social and political renewal.

These principles give a foundation for responsible political engagement, rather than mere (over)reaction. They give us a perspective beyond the next election and an independent stance that prevents us from being tucked into any political party's hip pocket. We must understand the biblical role of the state and then hold it accountable for fulfilling that role.

By this analysis, Jim Dobson is absolutely right in contending that Christians must oppose wickedness in high places—as they have in every age. A historical model is fourth-century Bishop Ambrose boldly confronting the Emperor Theodosius, who had ordered a brutal massacre of thousands of citizens in Thessalonica. Ambrose successfully demanded that the emperor do public penance. Another model, as Don Eberly notes, is the glorious Wilberforce-Shaftesbury era. Contemporary examples include the 1997 statement "We Hold These Truths," signed by some fifty Christian leaders, decrying the judicial usurpation of our democratic system, and the 1998 "Declaration Concerning Religion, Ethics, and the Crisis in the Clinton Presidency," signed by 157 theologians, calling on President Clinton to repent of the Lewinsky affair. As Jerry Falwell notes, the church is to be the conscience of society.

Of course, there are important distinctions between what is proper for the church as an institution and what is proper for the individual believer exercising his civic duty. The church can and should address moral issues (yes, from the pulpit), but it should never make partisan endorsements. It must not allow itself to be seduced by political power—something I saw all too often when I was in the White House. The church must guard its prophetic stance, leaving direct political activism to individual believers.

In addressing moral issues, moreover, we must not allow ourselves to be stereotyped. Cal Thomas correctly reminds us to address *every* issue from a Christian perspective—not only abortion and homosexual rights, but also poverty, social justice, and concern for the disenfranchised. I've spent twenty-five years working among the most marginalized people in society through a ministry to prison inmates, with a lobbying branch (Justice Fellowship) that advocates laws based on a biblical understanding of justice.

Above all, we must not succumb to despair. Jim Dobson, Jerry Falwell, and Ralph Reed all give stirring accounts of the impressive gains made by religious conservatives in the political arena. It is nothing short of astonishing that during the tenure of the most pro-abortion president in history, abortion rates are declining—largely because the pro-life message has pierced the public conscience. Don't believe the pessimists who say we can't change society.

As the new millennium approaches, the church can play a crucial role in restoring a culture mired in the anomie of postmodernism. Instead of being polarized by polemics, Christians ought to be charitable toward one another, constantly seeking common ground to work together in helping the church bring renewal to all the structures of God's creation.

Charles Colson is founder of Prison Fellowship and was special counsel to President Richard Nixon. Written with Nancy Pearcey, policy director of the Wilberforce Forum and executive editor of "Break Point," a daily radio commentary program featuring Charles Colson.

("What's Right About the Religious Right" was first published in *Christianity Today* on September 6, 1999.)

FAITH AND POLITICS AFTER THE RELIGIOUS RIGHT

An interview with Brian McLaren on the future of Christians in politics. Interviewed by Out of Ur, a weblog of *Leadership Journal*

In May 2007, the politically polarizing founder of the Moral Majority, Rev. Jerry Falwell, died. Falwell has been credited with mobilizing millions of evangelicals to engage the political process. The religious right, as the movement came to be called, has been a dominant political force ever since.

With the passing of Rev. Falwell, and with the 2008 presidential campaign gaining speed, some are wondering if the religious right will continue to hold its political power. Or, is a new form of Christian political engagement on the horizon? We sat down with Brian McLaren to discuss the political scene and how he believes the church should engage.

What encourages you, and discourages you, about the church and its involvement in the political realm?

My sense is that the religious right has hit its high tide. I think on a whole lot of levels it has been somewhat discredited. But I think the true believers in the religious right will go down with the ship, and I don't think they'll be willing to change their thinking no matter what happens. It's become a sort of ideology that has been absolutized and equated with gospel in their minds. I meet a number of people like this, and I like them but I can't imagine them changing. No amount of evidence will change them.

My big concern is that with the collapse of the religious right there isn't a mature and responsible Christian response that will fill the gap in a constructive way.

And I'm also concerned that the religious right will have left such a bad taste in the mouth of both the political world and the culture at large that there will be a reaction against any expression of faith in the public sphere. So this to me is a danger, but we have to do what we can.

What we should be asking is, how do we help our government be the kind of government that is pleasing to God? What I would hope is that people who are in the Republican Party who are followers of Jesus would use every bit of their energy and power to help the Republican Party reflect more and more the values of Jesus. And that Democrats who follow Jesus would do everything in their power to help the Democratic Party do the same thing more and more. Now in that way, you are actually more aligned, you're a stronger ally, with your fellow Christian in another party than you are with the people in the same party who have no higher allegiance than their partisan agenda.

So there should be a hierarchy of identity.

Exactly. A beautiful way to put it. But the sad thing is that in many cases because of this polarization of red and blue, liberal and conservative, left and right, people have shifted the hierarchy. So being a follower of Christ has become, in a way, a subset of being conservative or liberal.

You travel internationally quite a bit. Do you see a place where Christians are having that kind of positive impact on the government outside the United States?

Let me first say the same kind of religious right rhetoric happening here is being exported through religious broadcasting all over the world. I've been in countries where abortion is illegal and the church is constantly talking about it, even though it's already illegal, because they think this is what Christians are supposed to do because they hear it from the U.S. So it's strange. But to answer your question, yes, I do see it working out in powerful ways but most often in very local ways. In terms of national affairs I think it's a little harder to find, but that's also harder to do.

One of the issues I think we're really facing is that in the last sixteen hundred years we basically had three options. We've had the idea of the Holy Roman Empire where the church was the umbrella under which the state existed. And then in the Protestant era of civil religion the church existed to help the state achieve its goals. The third option makes the church into an isolated subculture where it withdraws from society and sees politics as dirty.

I think one of our great crises now is that we need a fourth option—a new option. It's an option that takes us back to the first three centuries of the church. I would call it more of a prophetic role. We often use prophetic to mean negative. It's thundering against sin. But the prophets were also poets, and a big part of what they did, as Walter Brueggemann says, is they funded the imagination with good possibilities. They created pictures—like swords being beaten into plowshares—that gave believers in God something to believe God for.

Prophets criticize and energize, I believe that's the way he put it.

Exactly. So we need that prophetic voice not just in the critical sense but also in the energizing sense. We have to imagine. We have to imagine what it would look like to have a nation where the gap between rich and poor was not so great. We have to imagine how that could happen in an equitable way. I'm not saying in a painless way. The fact is we have a lot of pain now. You always have pain. But at any rate, that to me is the role that the church needs to have.

And I think one of our terrible realizations is that in the first three-quarters of the twentieth century mainline Protestants were the civil religion of America and evangelicals were more the isolated subculture. Then I think we had a shift. So now evangelicals have become the civil religion of America and mainline Protestants feel like the isolated subculture. And now the question is, are we willing to look for a new option, a better option beyond the either/or's we've been stuck with.

Brian McLaren is a pastor and author. He is a columnist for *Leadership Journal* and is involved in emergent, Call to Renewal/Sojourners, and other innovative Christian organizations.

(This interview was published on the Web on Out of Ur (www.outofur.com) on June 14 and June 19, 2007. You can access the article and read the comments at http://blog.christianitytoday.com/outofur/archives/2007/06/faith_politics.html.)

Talking about politics is a tricky issue, especially when different opinions are raised. If you feel your group may need help navigating this issue and still *liking* each other at the end of your discussion, check out the Bonus Small-Group Builder on p.165. It provides great ideas for developing a group covenant to establish unity even during times of disagreement.

■ Open Up

Begin by taking 1 to 3 minutes for this short activity:

Politics are a polarizing topic in North America. In attempt to have a fair and congenial conversation, take a moment now for each group member to write a short list of all the negative assumptions and stereotypes they have about politics, political parties, politicians, and so on. When you're all finished with your lists, shoot them basketball style into a trash can. Try to keep your negative assumptions and comments in the trash can (literally and figuratively) as today's conversation progresses.

Now select one of the activities below to launch your discussion time.

Option 1

Discuss one of these icebreaker questions:

• Do you tend to keep your political views private or do you like to speak openly about them? Why? What has influenced your level of openness?

- When was the first time you took a strong political stand? How did others respond? Looking back, how do you feel about it now?

- Do you know committed Christians who have different political views than yourself? If so, what are your main areas of difference? If not, what's your general perspective on Christians who vote differently than you?

Option 2

People tend to think of politics on a rather simplified continuum that looks something like this:

Left	**Independent**	**Right**
Liberal	**Moderate**	**Conservative**

Generally speaking, where would you place *yourself* on this scale? Mark the spot with an X.

Once everyone's done, do your best to guess how each group member labeled themselves. Talk together about how your perceptions of each other's politics differed from or were consistent with the way you view yourselves.

■ The Issue

Politics is a volatile topic. And when political views are intimately tied to religious conviction, relationships can sometimes take the backseat to individual values and ideologies.

In today's articles, we read essays by two Christians who speak from different points on the political spectrum. Charles Colson would be viewed by many as a voice of the "Christian right" and Brian McLaren is generally considered to be a voice of the "Christian left," though both would say they're trying to be faithful to the Word of God and the example of Jesus.

- Based on these two articles, what are the main differences in perspective between McLaren and Colson? What is the common ground between them?

In "What's Right About the Religious Right," Colson encourages his readers to "develop a biblically grounded political philosophy that gets us off the pendulum and provides a basis for acting 'Christianly' in politics." He continues, "The classic elements of a Christian worldview—Creation, Fall, and Redemption—should guide our thinking."

- What are some public policies that reflect the Christian worldview of Creation, Fall, and Redemption?

- Select a political topic about which all members of the group do not agree. Some suggestions may include environmental protection/activism, capital punishment, welfare, or war. Discuss this topic from the framework of the Christian worldview. Even if you cannot agree on a solution, can you agree on the problem? Is this a helpful way for Christians to discuss politics?

■ Reflect

Take a moment to read **Matthew 5:43–48** and **Ephesians 4:1–5** on your own. Now write down ways you think these texts speak to the issue of political differences. What phrases seem most important? What issues do these raise for you in the realm of politics?

■ Let's Explore

God sets high standards for how we are to treat those with whom we disagree.

At some point or another, most of us have been in a political disagreement. Share stories about times you have felt alienated because of your political beliefs.

- How did this ultimately affect your relationship with the other individual?

- Do you have any relationships that are great despite significant political differences? If so, what makes this relationship work?

- Now, look at this from the other perspective. Have you ever treated someone badly or lambasted them for their different political views? How do you feel about this now?

Both **Matthew 5:43–48** and **Ephesians 4:1–5** give us direction on how we should treat those who are different from us. Re-read those passages; as you do, think about a relationship you have in which this direction would be beneficial.

- How can you balance strong political convictions in a personal relationship with someone of a different political view? What would this look like?

Not all political issues are black and white.

Colson admonishes the right to avoid centering itself on two issues: abortion and homosexual rights. Instead, he encourages Christians to equally consider issues of poverty, social justice, and the disenfranchised.

- Do you agree with Colson's caution here? Why or why not? How have you observed some pro-life, anti-gay agendas overshadow other human needs in this country?

- What encouraging things do you see Christians doing to combat this stereotype?

Often the polarizing rhetoric between conservatives and liberals leaves no room for alternate options. McLaren speaks about the need for this "new option" concerning Christian's involvements in politics. He encourages Christians to embrace a prophetic, imaginative voice that could energize society.

- Discuss a political issue that group members are interested in and concerned about, such as poverty, foreign relations, the oil crisis, or unemployment. Try to look at this issue from a new, imaginative angle and not take conventional "right" and "left" perspectives. What happens?

We are to trust in God, not any political system.

In our discussion of politics, it is imperative to remember that our membership is first in God's kingdom, not our country. However, often people of both political inclinations have a tendency to become sad (or worse) when considering all that is wrong in the world. However, Colson encourages his readers not to "succumb to despair."

- Have you ever despaired about the state of politics in your country? What was it that discouraged you?

- What has been your response when you have a sense of despair?

■ Going Forward

Break into pairs and discuss the following:

Both Colson and McLaren comment on the need for Christians on both sides of the political spectrum to align with one another. Colson specifically says, "be charitable toward one another, consistently seeking common ground to work together in helping the church bring renewal to all the structures of God's creation."

- What are ways Christians of different political opinions can work together for the good of God's kingdom? Brainstorm specific examples and ideas.

- How can you align yourself with (as opposed to against) other Christians politically? Share a concrete action you'd like to take.

When you have finished your discussion, gather together as a larger group and celebrate your unity in Christ by saying the Nicene Creed together (text below). Then pray together that in our highly politicized world, Christians will be unified by their common love for Christ.

The Nicene Creed

I believe in one God, the Father Almighty, Maker of heaven and earth, and of all things visible and invisible.

And in one Lord Jesus Christ, the only begotten Son of God, begotten of the Father before all worlds; God of God, Light of Light, very God of very God; begotten, not made, being of one substance with the Father, by whom all things were made.

Who, for us men and for our salvation, came down from heaven, and was incarnate by the Holy Spirit of the virgin Mary, and was made man; and was crucified also for us under Pontius Pilate; He suffered and was buried; and the third day He rose again, according to the Scriptures; and ascended into heaven, and sits on the right hand of the Father; and He shall come again, with glory, to judge the quick and the dead; whose kingdom shall have no end.

And I believe in the Holy Ghost, the Lord and Giver of Life; who proceeds from the Father and the Son; who with the Father and the Son together is worshipped and glorified; who spoke by the prophets.

And I believe in one holy catholic and apostolic Church. I acknowledge one baptism for the remission of sins; and I look for the resurrection of the dead, and the life of the world to come. Amen.

■ Want to Explore More?

Recommended Resources

Want to explore this topic further? Here are some resources that will help.

Beyond Left and Right: Helping Christians Make Sense of American Politics, Amy E. Black (Baker Books, 2008; ISBN 978-0-8010-6726-6).

Christian Perspectives on Politics, J. Philip Wogaman (Westminster John Knox, 2000; ISBN 978-0664222017)

Everything Must Change: Jesus, Global Crises, and a Revolution of Hope, Brian D. McLaren (Thomas Nelson, 2007; ISBN 0849901839)

God's Politics: Why the Right Gets it Wrong and the Left Doesn't Get It, Jim Wallis (HarperOne, 2006; ISBN 978-0060834470)

How Now Shall We Live? Charles Colson with Nancy Pearsey (Tyndale, 2004; ISBN 084235588X)

Red Letter Christians: A Citizen's Guide to Faith and Politics, Tony Campolo (Regal Books, 2008; ISBN 978-0830745296)

Is it possible to love your

country too much?

SCRIPTURE FOCUS

Romans 13:1–7

1 Peter 2:9–17

Revelation 5:9–10; 7:9

TRUE PATRIOTISM

■

The love of one's country is nothing new. For thousands of years, patriots have been willing to die for their country. How much do you love the place you call home? Since September 11, 2001 there has been an undeniable surge of American patriotism. In the weeks and months following that tragic day, a collective love of country was born that had not been experienced in a generation or two. This recent outpouring of patriotism has many Christians feeling caught in the crosshairs between faith and country.

This discussion will first focus on what the Apostles Paul and Peter say about the Christian's relationship to its government. Then we will take a deeper look into the *Christianity Today* article "What's Right About Patriotism" by David P. Gushee in which he delves into the issue of love of country and love for God.

■ Before You Meet

Read "What's Right About Patriotism" by David P. Gushee from *Christianity Today* magazine.

WHAT'S RIGHT ABOUT PATRIOTISM

The nation is not our highest love, but it still deserves our affection.

By David P. Gushee

My father used to display a crisp American flag outside of our house. That flag flew not just on holidays, but on every day of the year. He never told us why he flew the Stars and Stripes. It was not because he was obviously patriotic. Sure, he had served in the Korean War, but the experience sounded mainly harrowing. As an analyst for Congress, he was involved in the hurly-burly of public debate on major policy issues. He respected how our country's democratic system works. He was not sentimental about our nation. But he flew that flag every day.

Is it theologically appropriate for Christians to be patriotic? Does it compromise our citizenship in Christ's kingdom to wave the banner of loyalty to an earthly kingdom?

As with so many other issues, American Christians seem hopelessly divided.

On the Christian Right are many of that dwindling number of Americans who are happy to proclaim their love for this country and to wave the flag proudly as a symbol of that love. Meanwhile, on the Christian Left there is an emphasis on the international loyalties of Christ's people—and also some trenchant critiques of our nation's behavior. So the Right bashes the Left for its internationalism and critical spirit, while the Left skewers the Right for its confused consecration of national life.

Philosopher Jeffrey Stout says that piety is the virtue associated with gratitude toward the sources of one's existence. Love of country can, in this sense, be seen as a form of piety. We wave the flag in gratitude for the nation in which we live and move and have our being, the geographic source and arena of our existence. Asking someone to avoid patriotism because it compromises Christian faith is like asking them to avoid demonstrating affection to their parents because that, too, can compromise their Christian faith.

Abandoning patriotism can be a rejection of our embodiment as particular human beings in a particular context. It can mark a dismissal of the kinds of natural ties that root us to family, place, and time. I am here, not there; from these parents, not those parents; living in this era, not another one. I am not a free-floating spirit but an embodied person, rooted somewhere rather than nowhere. Patriotism simply says "thank you" for, and to, the particular national community in which our bodies have been placed.

Stepping Outside Ourselves

Thoughtful and usually progressive-minded Christians have expended much effort to steer us away from such patriotic sentiments. There are good reasons for this, many of them rooted in the grotesque horrors created by the exaggerated nationalism of the twentieth century. It is hard for any student of modern history not to think at least a bit about goose-stepping Nazi brownshirts whenever patriotism is mentioned.

Despite occasional feints in this direction during our nation's most desperate and fearful moments, nationalism of this type does not seem to be a serious threat today. Far more common is the inability to muster any kind of loyalty to any community outside the self and those few relationships that gratify the self.

Reinhold Niebuhr got it right in the early 1930s when he acknowledged that patriotism at least has the virtue of taking the self outside of itself to a broader community. Patriotism may be national egoism, as he called it, but it is an improvement over purely personal egoism, which can see no concern greater than the self.

It is deeply uncomfortable from a theological perspective that in many parts of our nation, the only place in which one can experience any substantive evocation of patriotism is the local Christian congregation. Other kinds of public celebrations of national loyalty have generally collapsed. What remains is—sometimes—a wordless local fireworks display down at the high school, which teaches us (I guess) that America can really do some spectacular explosives displays.

The church has a complicated task in relation to patriotism, and this collapse of any public space for patriotic displays makes that task all the harder. We need to be able to say "yes, but" to patriotism. Yes, we love our country, but we do not fully belong here or in any earthly land. Yes, we want our nation to flourish, but every human being and human community is equally precious in God's sight. Yes, we value our nation's ideals, but they are not the same thing as the message of the kingdom. Yes, God blesses America, but he blesses other nations, too.

Despite these concerns, it still seems to me that people who do not know how to demonstrate an appropriate fealty to their nation are not well-positioned to learn how to transcend that loyalty for a higher one.

David P. Gushee is Graves Professor of Moral Philosophy at Union University. His books include *Only Human: Christian Reflections on the Journey Toward Wholeness*; *Getting Marriage Right: Realistic Counsel for Saving and Strengthening Relationships*, and he is coauthor of *Kingdom Ethics: Following Jesus in a Contemporary Context*.

("What's Right About Patriotism" was first published in *Christianity Today*, July 2006, Vol. 50, No. 7.)

■ Open Up

Select one of these activities to launch your discussion time.

Option 1

Discuss one of these icebreaker questions:

- It is often said that it's impolite to discuss religion and politics. Why do you think this is? You may also want to tell about a time when a political discussion went sour.

- Have you ever traveled to another country? If yes, what was it like to be a political outsider? an American?

- If you consider yourself to be patriotic, how do you show it?

Option 2

Let's see if your patriotism is matched by your knowledge of American history. Take the following quiz as a group:

- Do you know all the words of the Pledge of Allegiance? Recite it.

- Do you know the lyrics to "The Star-Spangled Banner"? Sing or recite it.

- Can you name the first five Presidents?

- What were the thirteen original colonies?

(Answers are on p.65 at the end of the study.)

■ The Issue

In his article, David Gushee proposes that patriotism is love and care for your country of origin and that followers of Jesus can and should be patriotic because it serves as a model for devotion to God's kingdom.

- What does it mean to you to be patriotic?

- Name together some of the positive effects of patriotism as well as some of the negative ramifications of patriotism.

■ Reflect

Take a moment to read **Romans 13:1–7; 1 Peter 2:9–17** and **Revelation 5:9–10; 7:9** on your own. Write down anything that stands out to you or questions you may have regarding the passages. At first glance, how do these passages relate to patriotism? Take note of your observations.

■ Let's Explore

There will always be a tension between honoring our authorities and being exiles in our own country.

Read **1 Peter 2:11.** Here Peter describes followers of Jesus as being "sojourners and pilgrims." Other Bible translations use these words to describe our position on earth: exiles, aliens, temporary residents, pilgrims, and sojourners.

- What does it mean to be an exile or foreigner in your own nation? In what ways have you experienced this?

Peter and Paul each make the point that human authority is established by God, and we must submit to and obey that authority. Read **Romans 13:1–2** and **1 Peter 2:13–14.**

- What does that type of obedience look like today? Share specific examples.

- If we are exiles here on earth, is there room for patriotism in the Christian life? Do you think it is more important that we are exiles or that we are patriots? Why?

- Do you personally identify more with the exile or the patriot? Why?

Honoring our authorities can be taken too far when patriotism clouds the mission of the church.

- Do you feel America is a "Christian nation"? Should it be? Why or why not?

In his article, Gushee says, "It is deeply uncomfortable from a theological perspective that in many parts of our nation, the only place in which one can experience any substantive evocation of patriotism is the local Christian congregation. Other kinds of public celebrations of national loyalty have generally collapsed."

- Have you observed patriotism in church? If so, describe it. Do you believe promoting patriotism is part of the duty of the church? Why or why not?

Re-read both **Romans 13:1–7** and **1 Peter 2:9–17.** Here both Paul and Peter encourage believers to be citizens who respect their authorities, but the Apostles never mandate the church to publicly demonstrate allegiance to the Roman Empire.

- In your opinion, where should the church draw the line between its spiritual mandate to bring Jesus to the nations and its role as a government-recognized organization?

Our ultimate allegiance is to the kingdom of God.
Toward the end of his article, Gushee writes:

We need to be able to say "yes, but" to patriotism. Yes, we love our country, but we do not fully belong here or in any earthly land. Yes, we want our nation to flourish, but every human being and human community is equally precious in God's sight. Yes, we value our nation's ideals, but they are not the same thing as the message of the kingdom. Yes, God blesses America, but he blesses other nations, too.

- Explain the tension you may feel in your daily life between the values of your nation and the values of the kingdom of God.

Read **Revelation 5:9–10** and **7:9**. John makes a point here that people from every tribe, tongue, and nation make up the kingdom of God.

- Some Christians assert that patriotism—which generally views one's own country and people as superior to other nations or people groups—is completely contrary to the globally minded perspective God desires for his people. What do you think? Should Christians reject patriotism for this reason? Why or why not?

- With Revelation 5:9–10 and 7:9 in mind, how can you be patriotic while saying "yes, but" as Gushee suggests? What changes might this require in one's mind-set and actions?

- What does true patriotism to the kingdom of God look like in your daily life?

■ Going Forward

Take a minute to read and reflect on the following quote:

"There is a valid place for sensible patriotism. But from a Christian point of view, true patriotism acknowledges God's sovereignty over all the nations, and holds a healthy respect for God's judgment on the pretensions of any power that seeks to impose its will on others."
—Walter Wink, *Engaging the Powers*

- What do you think about Wink's assertion? Why?

Break into pairs for these final questions:

- In what ways do you feel God wants you to love your country? What might distinguish this type of love from common expressions of patriotism?

- Do you feel your life is more focused on this nation and its values or on God's kingdom and its values? What changes do you need to make?

Gather back together as a group to spend time praying for world leaders. Pray that they would use their power wisely and that God's will would be done throughout the world. Pray also for the spread of the gospel to "every tribe, language, people, and nation."

■ Want to Explore More?

Recommended Resources

Want to explore this topic further? Here are some resources that will help.

Web Articles

"Is Patriotism Dead?" a *Christianity Today* editorial, available at http://www.christianitytoday.com/ct/2001/julyweb-only/7-2-24.0.html

"Watching My Daughter 'Defect'" by Kenneth S. Kantzer in *Christianity Today*, available at http://www.christianitytoday.com/ct/2001/julyweb-only/7-2-26.0.html?start=1

Books

Engaging the Powers: Discernment and Resistance in a World of Domination, Walter Wink (Fortress Press, 1992; ISBN 0-8006-2646-X)

God's Politics: Why the Right Gets It Wrong and the Left Doesn't Get It, Jim Wallis (HarperOne, 2005; ISBN 0060558288)

God & Government, Charles W. Colson (Zondervan Publishing Company, 2007; ISBN 0310277647)

The Politics of Jesus, John Howard Yoder (William B. Eerdmans Publishing Company, 1972; ISBN 0-8028-0734-8)

Why Christians Should Not Pledge Allegiance to "One Nation Under God" by Michael J. Baxter from the book *God is Not . . . Religious, Nice, "One of Us," an American, a Capitalist,* edited by D. Brent Laytham (Brazos Press, 2004; ISBN 1-58743-101-7)

Christian Web Resources

http://www.aclj.org
http://www.citizenlink.org
http://www.sojourners.com

Quiz Answers

Pledge of Allegiance

I pledge allegiance to the flag of the United States of America, and to the republic for which it stands, one nation under God, indivisible, with liberty and justice for all.

The Star-Spangled Banner

O say, can you see, by the dawn's early light,
What so proudly we hailed at the twilight's last gleaming,
Whose broad stripes and bright stars, through the perilous fight,
O'er the ramparts we watched, were so gallantly streaming?
And the rockets' red glare, the bombs bursting in air,
Gave proof through the night that our flag was still there.
O say, does that star spangled banner yet wave
O'er the land of the free, and the home of the brave?

First Five American Presidents (in order)

George Washington, John Adams, Thomas Jefferson, James Madison, James Monroe

Original Thirteen Colonies

Connecticut, Delaware, Georgia, Maryland, Massachusetts, New Hampshire, New Jersey, New York, North Carolina, Pennsylvania, Rhode Island, South Carolina, Virginia

How can we labor for God's

kingdom during our time

here on earth?

SCRIPTURE FOCUS	
	Mark 2:13–17
	Acts 5:27–32
	Philippians 3:18–21
	1 Peter 2:13–21

DUAL CITIZENSHIP

■

September 11, 2001, was hardly the first time a vicious attack shook a predominantly Christian nation, writes Timothy George in his article "Theology for an Age of Terror." A few decades after the Roman Empire made Christianity its official religion—just as church leaders were gaining cultural power and social transformation seemed to be underway—an army of unbelievers reduced the "Eternal City" to ruins. Fifteen centuries later, as C. S. Lewis watched "Christian" Europe self-destruct, he pondered the same questions Augustine had asked in the last days of Rome: Why do so many promising human endeavors fail so miserably? Surrounded as we are by death and destruction, what can Christians possibly accomplish? How can we engage the world without being dragged down to its level? Is God's kingdom really coming? These are the questions we'll explore in this study.

■ Before You Meet

Read "Theology for an Age of Terror" by Timothy George from *Christianity Today* magazine.

THEOLOGY FOR AN AGE OF TERROR

Augustine's words after the 'barbarian' destruction of Rome have a remarkably contemporary ring.

By Timothy George

September 11, 2001, is frequently compared to December 7, 1941, as a day that will "live in infamy." But a more appropriate analogy might be August 24, 410, when the city of Rome was besieged and pillaged by an army of forty thousand "barbarians" led by the Osama bin Laden of late antiquity, a wily warrior named Alaric. One can still see the effects of this cataclysmic event when walking through the ruins of the Roman Forum today. The Basilica Aemilia was the Wall Street of ancient Rome, a beautiful structure in the Forum with a marble portico. One can still see the green stains of copper coins melted into the stone from the conflagrations set by Alaric and his marauders.

Before then, Roman coins bore the legend *Invicta Roma Aeterna*: eternal, unconquerable Rome. It had been more than eight hundred years since the Eternal City had fallen to an enemy's attack. In many ways, Rome was like America prior to 9/11, the world's only super-power. But in 410, Rome's military power could not prevent its walls being breached, its women raped, and its sacred precincts burned and sacked.

When Jerome heard about the fall of Rome in faraway Bethlehem, he put aside his *Commentary on Ezekiel* and sat stupefied in total silence for three days. "Rome was besieged," Jerome wrote to a friend. "The city to which the whole world fell has fallen. If Rome can perish, what can be safe?" The British monk Pelagius, who was in Rome when the attack occurred, gave this report: "Every household had its grief, and an all-pervading terror gripped us."

Responding to those who said Rome fell as the gods' punishment against the ascendant Christians, Augustine, the bishop of Hippo in North Africa, began writing *The City of God*, an *opus magnum et arduum*, as he called it—a "great and laborious work." Augustine completed the book shortly before his death in 430. Its influence extended to the Reformation and beyond. For fifteen hundred years, it has been the bedrock of a Christian philosophy of history.

Augustine's Journey

As a theologian in an age of terror, Augustine provides wisdom for our own precarious situation. Like C. S. Lewis, Augustine came to the Christian faith through a tortuous process of denial, doubt, false starts, dead ends, and surprising discovery. For nearly nine years, he followed the way of the Manicheans, radical dualists who divided the world into kingdoms of light and darkness and who taught that matter itself was inherently evil. Next he turned to academic skepticism. The skeptics, not unlike some postmodernists today, denied that there was any knowable absolute truth.

Later, he turned to Neo-Platonism, which offered a model of transcendence: It explained the world in terms of a spiritual reality—the ideals of truth, goodness, beauty—that could not be reduced to the flow and flux of the visible, changing world around us. Neo-Platonism continued to influence Augustine even after he became a Christian.

There were, however, two major problems with this philosophy that could not be squared with biblical faith. First, Neo-Platonism argued that matter had always existed. Creation was the work of an artisan who reshaped primordial matter into some other form. But the first five words of the Bible contradicted this cosmogony: "In the beginning God created." Augustine reflected deeply on the creation narrative in Genesis. In book 11 of *Confessions* he made a startling, brilliant discovery. He came to see that God had not only created both time and space, but that he had created them simultaneously and interdependently. (This insight, which Augustine derived from meditation on the Bible, anticipated Einstein's theory of relativity by fifteen hundred years.)

Second, Neo-Platonism had no explanation of history. The Christian doctrine of Creation does not mean merely that when God said "poof," the material cosmos popped into being. It means also that God is a principal actor in the unfolding drama of the world, its peoples, and its destiny. As John 1:14 puts it, "The Word became flesh and dwelt among us." Neo-Platonism had no place for the Incarnation, but Augustine came to see that this central datum of Christian revelation was the key to understanding the human story.

Between the conversion of Constantine in 312 and the conversion of Augustine in 386, the Christian movement had been transformed from a small, persecuted sect into a tolerated, then legally recognized, and finally officially established religion within the Roman Empire. While there were many benefits that came with this transformation, including the fact that Christians were no longer routinely hauled into the arena or fed to hungry lions, there was a downside as well.

Within a few generations, those who had once been persecuted became persecutors. For the first time, Christians had to think about what it means to follow Jesus Christ while also participating in civil governance. What does it mean to wage a just war? Can followers of a Palestinian peasant who declined to call armies of angels to deliver him from physical assault now sanction violence against heretics and recalcitrant pagans in his name?

Eusebius of Caesarea, the biographer of Constantine, had hailed the emperor as the thirteenth apostle and acclaimed his conversion in utopian terms. Nearly a century later, Augustine realized that such hopes were as misplaced as they had been premature. As wealthy refugees from Rome began to stream into Hippo with their horror stories of Alaric's acts—temples burned, women raped, citizens forced to flee for their lives—Augustine reminded his hearers that the City of God in its pilgrimage here on earth was not exempt from the ravages of time, that it was ever marked "by goading fears, tormenting sorrows, disquieting labors, and dangerous temptations."

Forgotten Distinction

With the assumptions of "Christendom" shaken again today by the forces of terror, Augustine teaches us that we must not equate any political entity—whether it be the Roman Empire, the American republic, the United Nations, or anything else—with the kingdom of God. Islam proclaims an undifferentiated understanding of the human community (*ummah*), whereas Christianity, especially in the Augustinian perspective, requires a proper respect for the complementary but clearly distinguishable roles of church and civil authority.

Whenever this distinction is forgotten or minimized, the Christian faith is in danger of being politicized and the state idolized. When this happens, religious liberty invariably gets trampled. The danger of being co-opted by forces inimical to the gospel is not limited to one political party or ideology. It can arise from any point along the political spectrum, from the raucous right, the loony left, or the mushy middle.

In the early 1930s, many earnest Christians in Germany equated the Nazi state with the direct unfolding of God's purpose in the world. In the face of this crisis, Karl Barth, Dietrich Bonhoeffer, and other courageous church leaders supported the Barmen Declaration. The first and second articles in this statement of faith argue for the supremacy of Jesus Christ over every temporal authority that would usurp the crown rights of the King of kings:

> Jesus Christ, as he has testified to us in the Holy Scripture, is the one Word of God whom we are to hear, whom we are to trust and obey in life and death. . . . Just as Jesus Christ is the pledge of the forgiveness of our sins, just so, and with the same earnestness, [he] is also God's mighty claim on the entirety of human life. In him we encounter a joyous liberation from the godless claims of this world to free and thankful service to its creatures.

This is one side of the Augustinian equation, but there is another. Christians hold a double citizenship in this world. Like the apostle Paul—who could claim that his true political identity was in heaven (Phil. 3:20), but who also appealed to Caesar as a Roman citizen when his life was at stake—so believers in Christ live as sojourners, resident aliens, in a world of profound discontinuity and frequently contested loyalty.

Jean Bethke Elshtain summarizes the counsel Augustine gives to believers beset by such fears and hopes: "Resisting altogether any notion of earthly perfection, Augustine offers instead a complex moral map that creates space for loyalty and love and care, as well as for a chastened form of civic virtue."

The key word here, *chastened*, calls for a posture of engagement that acknowledges, in the words of the old gospel hymn, "This world is not my home; I'm just a-passing through," while *at the same time* working with all our might to love our neighbors as ourselves and to seek justice and peace as we carry out what Augustine called "our business within this common mortal life."

There are two major (and regrettably common) mistakes Augustine wants us to avoid. One is the lure of utopianism. This is the mistake of thinking that we can produce a human society that will solve our problems and bring about the kingdom of God on earth. This was the basic error of both Marxism and nineteenth-century liberalism.

The other error, equally disastrous, is cynicism. This creeps up on us as we see ever-present evil. We withdraw into our own self-contained circle of contentment, which can just as well be a pious holy huddle as a secular skeptics club.

Fragile World, Strong Faith

How can we avoid such reactions? Perhaps another great Christian of the past, Francis of Assisi, can help. One day when Francis was riding to Assisi, he saw a leper on the road. He reached out to embrace the leper and actually gave him the kiss of peace. While embracing this filthy, diseased outcast, Francis said, he was overcome by a dual sensation. One was nausea. The other was a sense of sweetness and well-being. Like Francis, we need both.

If all we experience is nausea, we will become cynics. We will give up on the world and turn away. But if all we have is sweetness, then our faith will amount to little more than sentimental fluff.

Genuine Christian faith, and true ministry, takes place on the thin line between nausea and sweetness. Feel-good Christianity, so common in our popular culture, actually masks the suffering and pain of the world for which Christ died.

C. S. Lewis preached at the University Church of St. Mary the Virgin at Oxford on October 22, 1939. Less than two months earlier, Hitler had invaded Poland. Britain was about to face the horrible Nazi onslaught. This is what Lewis told the assembled students:

> It may seem odd for us to carry on classes, to go about our academic routine in the midst of a great war. What is the use of beginning when there is so little chance of finishing? How can we study Latin, geography, algebra in a time like this? Aren't we just fiddling while Rome burns?
>
> This impending war has taught us some important things. Life is short. The world is fragile. All of us are vulnerable, but we are here because this is our calling. Our lives are rooted not only in time, but also in eternity, and the life of learning, humbly offered to God, is its own reward. It is one of the appointed approaches to the divine reality and the divine beauty, which we shall hereafter enjoy in heaven and which we are called to display even now amidst the brokenness all around us.

That is our calling, too, amidst the brokenness—including the threat of terrorism—all around us. We are to be faithful to God's calling, to bear witness to the beauty, the light, and the divine reality that we shall forever enjoy in heaven. We are to do this in a culture that seems, at times, like Augustine's, a crumbling world beset by dangers we cannot predict.

As Augustine aged, he increasingly thought of the world, its politics, culture, and institutions, as a tottering old man whose days were numbered: "You are surprised that the world is losing its grip? That the world is grown old? Don't hold onto the old man, the world; don't refuse to regain your youth in Christ, who says to you: 'The world is passing away; the world is losing its grip; the world is short of breath. Don't fear, your youth shall be renewed as an eagle.'"

As Augustine lay dying in 430, a new wave of terror swept across the Mediterranean world. The Vandals, led by a ferocious warrior named Genseric, surrounded Hippo—bringing torture, violence, and disarray to its churches and its people. As Augustine chanted the psalms on his deathbed, he might have come across this verse in Psalm 31:21: "Blessed be the Lord, for He has shown me His marvelous kindness in a strong city!"

Timothy George is dean of Beeson Divinity School of Samford University and an executive editor of *Christianity Today*.

("Theology for an Age of Terror" was originally published in *Christianity Today*, September 2006.)

■ Open Up

Select one of these activities to launch your discussion time.

Option 1

- Imagine that for some reason you had to move to another country and become a citizen there. What country would you choose? Why would you want to be a citizen of that country? (Or, if you are a citizen of another country, share with the group how your home country compares with life here.)

- What rights do you most cherish as an American citizen (or a citizen of your home country)? Brainstorm together the most important rights that distinguish your citizenship from that of other nations.

The Declaration of Independence states: "We hold these truths to be self-evident, that all men are created equal, that they are endowed by their Creator with certain unalienable Rights, that among these are Life, Liberty and the pursuit of Happiness. — That to secure these rights, Governments are instituted among Men . . . "

- We often take these rights for granted without really thinking about how they affect our daily life. In what ways have you enjoyed the right to life, the right to liberty, and the right to pursue happiness? Brainstorm specific examples.

Option 2

What *are* your civil rights? Take a trip down memory lane to high school civics class and try to name together the basic ideas in the ten articles in the Bill of Rights. (See p.85 for a summary.)

- What do you see as the two or three most important rights in this document? Defend your view.

- If you had to give up two or three of these rights, which would you select? Why?

■ The Issue

Though hardly anyone talks about "Christendom" anymore, Timothy George suspects that many people believe in it. Augustine (354–430), one of the greatest theologians in the Western church, drew fine distinctions between God's kingdom and earthly powers in his monumental *City of God*, but Christians have struggled ever since to follow his guidance. At times, Christians have placed too much faith in human institutions, believing their church or nation to be God's perfect instrument. The results of this misplaced enthusiasm have always been disastrous. Some critics charge American evangelicals with making this mistake today. Any talk of America being a chosen nation or having a God-given mission in the world makes such critics intensely nervous.

George warns against the opposite mistake as well. Christians face a temptation to eschew civic activity in order to evade worldly contamination. In these situations, George writes, "We withdraw into our own self-contained circle of contentment, which can just as well be a pious holy huddle as a secular skeptics club." American evangelicals get accused of committing this error, too, when they shun interfaith endeavors and preach against other people's sins. Some observers charge that evangelicals are thoroughly *of* the world—selfish, materialistic, power-hungry—even as they marshal all of their suburban resources to avoid being *in* it.

- Why is it so hard for Christians to find the right balance between the demands of earthly citizenship and those of heavenly citizenship? What specific situations seem to put these demands in conflict?

■ Reflect

Take a moment to read **Mark 2:13–17; Acts 5:27–32; Philippians 3:18–21;** and **1 Peter 2:13–21** on your own. Write down a few notes and observations about the passages: What stands out to you as the main idea in each passage? What questions do these passages raise?

■ Let's Explore

We must distinguish between our citizenship in God's kingdom and our obligations toward our earthly kingdom.
Read **Philippians 3:18–21.**

• What does it mean to you to live as a citizen of God's kingdom? What rights and privileges does your citizenship entail? What "laws" of the kingdom govern your daily life?

With reference to Augustine, George writes, "we must not equate any political entity—whether it be the Roman Empire, the American republic, the United Nations, or anything else—with the kingdom of God." Augustine also cautioned against equating the visible church with the kingdom. The kingdom is perfect, eternal, and ruled by a holy God, while even the best earthly institutions are imperfect, changing, and governed—proximately, if not ultimately—by fallible human beings.

George goes on to say that, "Christianity, especially in the Augustinian perspective, requires a proper respect for the complementary but clearly distinguishable roles of church and civil authority. Whenever this distinction is forgotten or minimized, the Christian faith is in danger of being politicized and the state idolized. When this happens, religious liberty invariably gets trampled. The danger of being co-opted by forces inimical to the gospel is not limited to one political party or ideology. It can arise from any point along the political spectrum, from the raucous right, the loony left, or the mushy middle."

- What are some examples you've observed of Christians today forgetting to distinguish between church and civil authority? How have you observed Christian faith being politicized? Or in what ways have you seen Christians "idolize" the state?

George mentions Eusebius of Caesarea, a pastor and biographer of Rome's first Christian emperor, Constantine. Eusebius had endured the last great persecution of Christians in the empire before living to see a fellow believer in command of the realm. The sudden change of fortune overwhelmed him, leading him to write, in 337, excessive praise of the lately deceased emperor:

> But now, while I desire to give utterance to some of the customary sentiments, I stand perplexed and doubtful which way to turn, being wholly lost in wonder at the extraordinary spectacle before me. For to whatever quarter I direct my view, whether to the east, or to the west, or over the whole world, or toward heaven itself, everywhere and always I see the blessed one yet administering the self-same empire. On earth I behold his sons, like some new reflectors of his brightness, diffusing everywhere the luster of their father's character, and himself still living and powerful, and governing all the affairs of men more completely than ever before, being multiplied in the succession of his children. They had indeed had previously the dignity of Caesars; but now, being invested with his very self, and graced by his accomplishments, for the excellence of their piety they are proclaimed by the titles of Sovereign, Augustus, Worshipful, and Emperor.

Elation about the end of persecution caused Eusebius to overlook Constantine's many sins, which included ordering the execution of his wife and oldest son, and to gloss over the political divisions already threatening the Roman Empire. Eusebius saw only what he wanted to see, and he staked his future on it.

- Imagine you were having a conversation with Eusebius—a pastor and your brother in Christ. What would you say to him? In your opinion, how should Eusebius have viewed Constantine and his empire?

- How does your advice to Eusebius speak to Christians today and the way we relate to governing authorities? How does your advice speak to you personally?

Despite their flaws, human governing institutions play key roles in God's plan.

The Roman Empire around the time of Constantine remains a source of much debate in Christian circles. Before Constantine, the empire persecuted Christians, yet church leaders at the time refrained from calling the government evil or advising Christians to overthrow it. Under Constantine and his immediate successors, the Roman government sought to further what it understood to be the goals of the church. This meant funding church-building campaigns and generally cleaning up society, but it also meant intervening in theological debates, prosecuting heretics, and waging war in God's name. Less than a century after Constantine, the empire was weakened by dissension—among Christians, and between Christians and members of other religions—and, finally, crushed by invaders.

Eusebius and most of his contemporaries saw Constantine's conversion as an unmistakable turn for the better. Some Christians in more recent centuries consider the Constantinian alliance between church and state to be a trap from which true Christianity has struggled ever since to escape. Similarly, the fall of the empire was viewed by most Romans as a bitter and shocking catastrophe, while various later observers have seen it as an inevitable, though lamentable, consequence of poor political planning or as a divine blow enabling the church to renew its real mission. Augustine could only be sure that God knew all about the Romans' successes and failures and that his kingdom was bigger than any of them. This assurance is based in Scripture.

Exodus details the account of God's miraculous work to free his people from slavery in Egypt. It provides great hope of God's deliverance. But 1 Peter 2:13–21 presents a very different picture of life under a harsh foreign power. Peter promises no escape or earthly deliverance; he gives no indication of what God is doing "behind the scenes."

- Peter wrote these words to Christians living under the hostile rule of pagan and Jewish authorities. They would have remembered Herod's slaughter of baby boys (Matthew 2:13–18), Jesus's crucifixion, and numerous other atrocities not detailed in the New Testament. Yet Peter counsels obedience. Which elements in this passage conflict with American notions of freedom, democracy, and equality?

- Peter advises in verse 17, "Honor all people. Love the brotherhood. Fear God. Honor the King." What different behaviors (from the passage and your own experience) fit under the headings "love," "respect," and "honor"? Are these different types or levels of obedience?

- How might this passage strike believers living in countries like China, Iraq, or, at the opposite extreme, the super-tolerant Netherlands?

- Are American Christians modeling what they should be modeling in this area? Explain.

Civil society can be a dangerous place, but Christians are needed there.

Near the end of his article, George writes of a "chastened form of civic virtue," explaining: "The key word here, *chastened*, calls for a posture of engagement that acknowledges, in the words of the old gospel hymn, 'This world is not my home; I'm just a-passing through,' while *at the same time* working with all our might to love our neighbors as ourselves and to seek justice and peace as we carry out what Augustine called 'our business within this common mortal life.'" That posture of engagement can take a variety of forms.

- In his Sermon on the Mount, Jesus taught that his followers are to be "salt" and "light" in this world (see Matthew 5:13–16). But Jesus didn't explain what he meant or provide examples of what this should look like in everyday life. What other stories and teachings in Scripture point you toward what it means to live as salt and light? What are some contemporary examples of this you've seen in the realm of politics and government?

Read **Mark 2:13–17.** Evangelicals tend to think of social problems in individual terms: poverty, domestic abuse, addiction, and so forth are fought one changed heart at a time. The call of Levi, recorded in Mark 2, certainly changed his life. But Levi was not just a crooked man—he was a cog in a corrupt tax-collecting machine. By virtue of his job, he was *part* of an unjust governing system.

- How, then, did Levi's conversion also have broader social implications? Was there value in the dinner at Levi's house, even if no one other than Levi came to Christ through it?

Read **Acts 5:27–32.** Here it seems that Peter is disobeying his own advice (in 1 Peter 2:13–21). He declares, "We ought to obey God rather than men" (Acts 5:29).

- How can you reconcile the apparent contradiction? What does this example teach us about engaging civic authority? In what circumstances should our engagement take the form of direct confrontation or active resistance to human authority?

■ Going Forward

Break into pairs to discuss the next two questions:

George tells a story about St. Francis of Assisi. Re-read that story together (the first two paragraphs under the subhead "Fragile World, Strong Faith" on p.72).

- What's your response to this story? Share an example of a time you've felt both "nausea" and "sweetness" about an issue in our culture or an action of our government?

- George poses utopianism and cynicism as equal and opposite dangers for Christians. When it comes to the government, which is the bigger danger for your church? For you personally? Why?

Gather back together as a group.

Ultimately, for Augustine, specific political involvements—or non-involvement—mattered less than the disposition of the heart. Read this quote:

> Two cities have been formed by two loves: the earthly by the love of self, even to the contempt of God; the heavenly by the love of God, even to the contempt of self. The former, in a word, glories in itself, the latter in the Lord. For the one seeks glory from men; but the greatest glory of the other is God, the witness of conscience. The one lifts up its head in its own glory; the other says to its God, "Thou art my glory, and the lifter up of mine head." In the one, the princes and the nations it subdues are ruled by the love of ruling; in the other, the princes and the subjects serve one another in love, the latter obeying, while the former take thought for all. The one delights in its own strength, represented in the persons of its rulers; the other says to its God, "I will love Thee, O Lord, my strength."

Christians may legitimately disagree about the role of governments in the world or about the role of Christians in government, but none can dispute that the eternal, infallible God must be our glory and strength.

- What stands out to you most from Augustine's words? What do you love about God and his kingdom? What has being a citizen of God's kingdom brought to your life?

Pray together, praising God as the ultimate King in your life and thanking him for the blessing of being a citizen in his kingdom. Ask God to give you wisdom in navigating the tough issues of "dual citizenship."

■ Want to Explore More?

Recommended Resources

Want to explore this topic further? Here are some resources that will help.

Christian History issue 67: Augustine (http://www.christianitytoday.com/ch/2000/003/)

Broken We Kneel: Reflections on Faith and Citizenship, Diana Butler Bass (John Wiley & Sons, 2004; ISBN 0787972843)

City of God, Augustine (selections), see http://www.fordham.edu/halsall/source/aug-city2.html

The Gospel of the Kingdom: Scriptural Studies in the Kingdom of God, George Eldon Ladd (Eerdmans, 1959; ISBN 0802812805)

The Kingdom of Christ: The New Evangelical Perspective, Russell D. Moore (Crossway, 2004; ISBN 1581346271)

Uneasy Neighbors: Church and State in the New Testament, Walter E. Pilgrim (Augsburg/Fortress Press, 1999; ISBN 0800631137)

The Bill of Rights

Amendment 1: Congress shall make no law respecting an establishment of religion, or prohibiting the free exercise thereof; or abridging the freedom of speech, or of the press; or the right of the people peaceably to assemble, and to petition the government for a redress of grievances.

Amendment 2: A well regulated militia, being necessary to the security of a free state, the right of the people to keep and bear arms, shall not be infringed.

Amendment 3: No soldier shall, in time of peace be quartered in any house, without the consent of the owner, nor in time of war, but in a manner to be prescribed by law.

Amendment 4: The right of the people to be secure in their persons, houses, papers, and effects, against unreasonable searches and seizures, shall not be violated, and no warrants shall issue, but upon probable cause, supported by oath or affirmation, and particularly describing the place to be searched, and the persons or things to be seized.

Amendment 5: No person shall be held to answer for a capital, or otherwise infamous crime, unless on a presentment or indictment of a grand jury, except in cases arising in the land or naval forces, or in the militia, when in actual service in time of war or public danger; nor shall any person be subject for the same offense to be twice put in jeopardy of life or limb; nor shall be compelled in any criminal case to be a witness against himself, nor be deprived of life, liberty, or property, without due process of law; nor shall private property be taken for public use, without just compensation.

Amendment 6: In all criminal prosecutions, the accused shall enjoy the right to a speedy and public trial, by an impartial jury of the state and district wherein the crime shall have been committed, which district shall have been previously ascertained by law, and to be informed of the nature and cause of the accusation; to be confronted with the witnesses against him; to have compulsory process for obtaining witnesses in his favor, and to have the assistance of counsel for his defense.

Amendment 7: In suits at common law, where the value in controversy shall exceed twenty dollars, the right of trial by jury shall be preserved, and no fact tried by a jury, shall be otherwise reexamined in any court of the United States, than according to the rules of the common law.

Amendment 8: Excessive bail shall not be required, nor excessive fines imposed, nor cruel and unusual punishments inflicted.

Amendment 9: The enumeration in the Constitution, of certain rights, shall not be construed to deny or disparage others retained by the people.

Amendment 10: The powers not delegated to the United States by the Constitution, nor prohibited by it to the states, are reserved to the states respectively, or to the people.

■ Notes

Has the nation finally abandoned its Judeo-Christian heritage, or are we still making great strides for Christ?

SCRIPTURE FOCUS	Deuteronomy 21:1–9
	Isaiah 8:11–22
	Matthew 13:24–30, 36–43

AMERICA: A NATION OF PAGANS OR CHRISTIANS?

■

It is an oft-repeated observation in churches that the United States is no longer a Christian nation, if it ever really was. But there's also no question that Christianity looms large in our culture. On the one hand, Christians think that this culture has abandoned its Christian roots almost entirely and believers must now act as spiritual guerillas, infiltrating the culture undercover to do what we can to stave off inevitable collapse. On the other hand, we think that Christianity still has enormous positive influence in our culture and we should take heart that our salt still seasons society and our light still shines from a hill. This study evaluates these two contrasting views, based on articles in *Christianity Today* by Harold O. J. Brown and Leith Anderson.

■ Before You Meet

Read "The Christian Future of America: Two Views" by Leith Anderson and Harold O.J. Brown from *Christianity Today* magazine.

THE CHRISTIAN FUTURE OF AMERICA: TWO VIEWS

Has the nation finally abandoned its Judeo-Christian heritage, or is there still hope?

By Leith Anderson and Harold O. J. Brown

Recent events have left Christians wondering how they stand in American society. In the last year, we at *Christianity Today* have received several manuscripts by prominent Christian intellectuals suggesting that the United States has become definitively and irreversibly anti-God. Other Christians continue to urge us to do good with the hope that we can make a difference. Each side can marshal compelling arguments and strong evidence. Here we publish two views on the matter by two prominent evangelical leaders.

Harold O. J. Brown has led a distinguished academic career and now serves as a professor of theology at Reformed Theological Seminary in Charlotte, North Carolina. He is the author of many books, most recently *The Sensate Culture* (Word, 1996), and as the editor of *The Religion and Society Report,* Professor Brown has relentlessly exposed the folly of Western society's anti-life drift.

Leith Anderson is pastor of Wooddale Church in Eden Prairie, Minnesota. Anderson is one of the most respected pastors and leaders in America, having also served as interim president of Denver Seminary and the National Association of Evangelicals. He is the author of many books, most recently *Leadership That Works: Hope and Direction for Church and Parachurch Leaders in Today's Complex World* (Bethany, 2002).

The following two articles came to us separately. The authors did not see each other's manuscripts ahead of time, and so are not debating one another. Nor are these essays intended to be finely reasoned theological or sociological arguments. While they offer arguments, they distill moods shaped by the authors' years of passionate involvement in trying to shape American culture for Christ.

—The Editors

A STEADY CHRISTIAN INFLUENCE

By Leith Anderson

I spoke at a convention in Philadelphia where, after one of my sessions, a woman raised her hand and asked, "If the gospel and the church are supposed to be so effective, why is everything in America so bad?"

What she was saying, basically, is that the gospel of Jesus Christ doesn't work. And perhaps the reason she assumes that failure is because she has heard that message so often from our pulpits, our broadcasts, and our publications. The gospel might have worked somewhere else. It might have worked at another time. But we are repeatedly told that the gospel doesn't work anymore; we have had ample opportunity in America for the gospel to have significant impact, but what we often hear is that things are getting far worse.

So how bad are things in the United States? Indeed, we live in difficult times. Not one of us needs to look very far to see the effects of sin. We have corporate corruption, pornography, abortions, divorces, anemic churches, five million couples living together who are not married, clergy immorality, drug abuse, and more.

But that really isn't anything new, is it? In the history of America, the roots of deism and secularism go back a long way. Books like *Undaunted Courage,* about the Lewis and Clark expedition, and *Theodore Rex,* the biography of Theodore Roosevelt, remind us of the appalling immorality, drug abuse, and business and political corruption that permeated generations one hundred and two hundred years ago.

So things have been bad, and continue to be bad, in lots of ways. But what kind of influence are Christians having on our country today?

The Difference We Make

One hundred and fifty years ago, slavery became illegal in America when abolitionist Christians put their lives on the line for human freedom. One hundred years ago in America, opium, laudanum (an opium-based painkiller), and morphine use was so pervasive that it produced an unprecedented number of addicts. One hundred years ago, the Sears and Roebuck catalog sold heroine and syringes through the mail. Fifty years ago theological liberalism dominated the religious landscape of America, and born-again Christians were clearly on the margins of society.

Today, those who publicly state that they are born-again Christians include the President of the United States, the attorney general, the national security adviser, governors of many states, members of Congress, senators, CEOs of our largest corporations, university professors, bestselling authors like John Grisham, country music stars like Randy Travis—on and on the list goes.

New York City had a reputation a generation ago for being one of the dirtiest and most unsafe cities in the world. Today it has one of the lowest crime rates, per capita, in the country. More than three-quarters of Americans describe themselves as Christians. Churches where the Bible is taught and holiness is lived are multiplying and flourishing. The largest and most effective churches in America, almost without exception, have a serious commitment to the truth of the Bible and the authority of Jesus Christ.

There are fewer R-rated films produced now than there were ten years ago. And one of the most successful R-rated films is *The Passion of the Christ*. The bestselling books in America, and around the world, in recent years have included *The Prayer of Jabez, Left Behind*, and *The Purpose-Driven Life*.

I remember well when pornography magazines were sold in 7-Eleven and other convenience stores. I don't recommend that you go and look for them, but you would have difficulty finding those publications readily available in those stores today.

The New York Times editorialized recently that evangelical Christians in America are shaping U.S. foreign policy toward righteousness.

And on it goes. Christians are living holy lives that are having an enormous impact within our society.

Some Christian leaders say that Christianity in America is, in fact, three thousand miles wide and one inch deep. As someone who travels a great deal in this country and interacts across the nation on a weekly basis with Christians, I simply say, that's not my experience.

One way to test that theory is to take out the sharp knife of tragedy and cut deep to see what's under an inch of American Christianity. I remember the day of tragedy at Columbine High School. My wife, Charleen, and I walked the perimeter of the fence and saw the thousands upon thousands of notes and little shrines that were established. We spent hours reading them, and almost all of them acknowledged a loyalty to God and a love for Jesus Christ.

I was commuting to a job in Washington, D.C., when the sniper tragedies were taking lives at random around the metropolitan area. And I watched carefully on television when people who were absolutely shaken by the tragic deaths of family members stated that their only hope and confidence was in Jesus Christ and that Jesus Christ had given them strength, stability, and peace in the midst of their difficulties.

September 11, 2001, produced more testimonies to Jesus Christ than anything that I can remember in recent times.

On September 29 of last year, there was a shooting in a Hennepin County Courthouse in the Twin Cities in Minnesota. A severely wounded attorney lay bleeding on the floor of the courthouse hallway. The *Minneapolis Star Tribune* in a front-page story told about the woman who knelt down in front of this man. She pressed her navy blue suit jacket so hard against the wound on his neck that her arm shook. "Jesus, please save this man," she prayed over and over. "Jesus, don't let this man die."

We often hear cynical Christians condemn the impotence of American Christianity, but listen to a real cynic: Justin Webb, the BBC correspondent in Washington, D.C. He spoke about his postings in Belgium, London, and then the United States:

> My wife and I do not believe in God. In our last posting, in Brussels among the nominally Catholic Belgians, unbelief was not a problem. . . .

Our house in London was right next to a church. We talked to the tiny congregation about the weather, about the need to prune the rose-bushes and mend the fence, but we never talked about God.

How different it is here on this side of the Atlantic. . . . I am not talking about the Bible Belt—or about the loopy folk who live in log cabins in Idaho and Oregon and worry that the government is poisoning their water. I'm talking about Mr. and Mrs. Average in Normal Town, U.S.A. Mr. and Mrs. Average share an uncomplicated faith with its roots in the Puritanism of their forbears. According to that faith there is such a thing as heaven—86 percent of Americans, we are told by the pollsters, believe in heaven.

But much more striking for me and much more pertinent to current world events is that 76 percent, or three out of four people you meet on any American street, believe in hell and the existence of Satan. They believe the devil is out to get you, that evil is a force in the world—a force to be engaged in battle. Much of the battle takes place in the form of prayer. Americans will talk of praying as if it were the most normal, rational thing to do. The jolly plump woman who delivers our mail in the Washington suburbs has a son who is ill—the doctors are doing their best, she says, but she's praying hard and that's what will do the trick.

And so I'll tell you, I'm awed. I'm impressed and awed by Christians in America who when facing unexpected tragedies turn to God.

Growing Wheat

Jesus's parable of the wheat and the weeds in Matthew 13 is fitting for us who live in the best of times and the worst of times. Servants asked the master whether they should tear out the weeds that had unexpectedly grown up alongside the wheat. The master replied no: "Because while you are pulling the weeds you may root up the wheat with them. Let both grow together until the harvest. At that time I will tell the harvesters, first collect the weeds and tie them into bundles to be burned and then gather the wheat and bring it into my barn."

Let there be no doubt, wheat and weeds are growing side by side in America. But Jesus tells his followers not to worry about pulling up the weeds—he will take care of that later. Instead he tells his followers to grow the wheat.

A DECISIVE TURN TO PAGANISM

By Harold O. J. Brown

From all that terror teaches, from lies of tongue and pen,
From all the easy speeches that comfort cruel men,
From sale and profanation of honor and the sword,
From sleep and from damnation, deliver us, good Lord.
—G. K. Chesterton

Our nation has lived for three decades with what must be the greatest lie "of tongue and pen" of the twentieth century, handed solemnly down by seven unelected justices of the U.S. Supreme Court: "We do not know when human life begins." The conclusion that the justices drew in *Roe v. Wade* was unwarranted, namely, because if we say that we do not know whether human life has begun, we may allow its termination at any time up to the undeniable birth of a live baby. Now, three decades later, we have perhaps 42 million fewer Americans, of which perhaps 15 or 16 million would be between the ages of eighteen and thirty today. The lie must comfort the cruel men—and the women too, now—who give us leave to terminate life prior to birth, at will.

While our nation plans great things for the world—democracies in the Middle East, peace between Israel and the Palestinians, no more weapons of mass destruction (other than in our own hands or in the hands of those too powerful for us to oppose), prescription drugs for older people, no child left behind (of those who succeed in being born)—the number of us who will enjoy those great things is declining, thanks in large part to abortion, as European and American births drop below the replacement rate.

What is going on here? In his 1978 Harvard Commencement address, Aleksandr Solzhenitsyn uttered words that have made him forever politically incorrect: "Men have forgotten God." In the United States, a large majority of the population is associated with Christianity, and a substantial minority calls itself practicing, observant, evangelical, born again, or otherwise conservatively Christian. God is not forgotten on

Sunday, not in the churches, great and small, that dot the landscape. But otherwise?

What happened immediately after *Roe v. Wade?* Christians seemed to have fled to the catacombs, caves, or foxholes, for they were hardly in evidence. The anti-abortion efforts of the Roman Catholic laity put its episcopate to shame; Protestants, used to thinking of their nation as mildly Christian, did little, until the late Francis Schaeffer stirred evangelicals with his film series, *Whatever Happened to the Human Race?*

To be sure, the number of Christians now stirred up includes more than one in the high halls of power, and occasionally pious bleats are heard. But still at least one-quarter of those awaiting birth are destroyed, "safely and legally," during the nine months of pregnancy.

The fact that *Roe,* a clear repudiation of the biblical Judeo-Christian teaching that each human is made in the image of God, did not lead to a massive rejection of the Court and its allies has shown our judges and justices that they may not only forget God, they may install idols in his place.

Roe is now history. It is part of the furniture, as Justice Sandra Day O'Connor would put it. Now something far more important for the future of Christianity in the United States, and by implication for the future of the entire country and its people, has taken place.

A Ruling for Paganism

On July 8, 2003, the United States Supreme Court, by a vote of 6–3 (in *Lawrence v. Texas*) did not merely forget God: It turned the nation into a pagan state—not the people, of course, not all the lesser structures and institutions such as churches, schools, and businesses great and small, but the nation. The Supreme Court, in declaring all sodomy laws unconstitutional, has in effect declared the nation pagan—not in so many words, of course, but in terms that explicitly repudiate historic Christianity, the Bible, the Torah, and the principles of natural law that guided us so long.

The Court did not, of course, declare the legislature (i.e. Congress, the administration, the President, and his cabinet) pagan. It could not do so. Congress has Christian members, Catholics and Protestants, and Jewish members, some even observant and orthodox. The President and some members of his administration are Christians, some outspokenly so. But the nation, which has been slowly losing its Christianity, has now been in essence declared pagan, and all its institutions, agencies, and departments will follow, gradually or speedily.

Lawrence passed by a two-thirds majority. What were those justices thinking? The man who wrote the majority opinion is a Roman Catholic. Does he not know that his church, his spiritual leader the pope, the Bible, and all of the church fathers up to the present, consider the behavior that he now protects an abominable sin, an act against nature? Was it a trivial matter to award the highest court's protection to activities against nature and the laws of God and the church? Do the two Jewish justices not know that their Torah rejects sodomy as an abomination? And the two women on the Court: By what perverted logic do they mock the role that God and nature have given to their sex in conjunction with the male—to bring children into the world in a matrimonial union—to support this perverse caricature of the purpose of sex and with it the negation of the irreplaceable role of their sex in the survival of our human race? The logic of *Lawrence* implicitly steers toward the dying off of the human race, or at least of such parts of it as are guided by our high court.

By this tortured reasoning, if we can call it that, the God of Abraham, Isaac, Jacob, and Moses, the God and Father of our Lord Jesus Christ, has been banned from the scene in the nation whose endeavors he has so often blessed. In his place we have, if anything, the gods of Sodom and Gomorrah. The justices, in their sovereign bliss, with the exception of the dissenters, do not seem to know what they have done. Or do they know and not care? Or know and want to do exactly what they have done?

Those of us who do see and know what has been done must not wait until all of the organs of government are brought under the gods of Sodom: We must look, see, and speak. We cannot change the Court's decision, not now and perhaps not ever, but we can and must say with the Israelites of the past, regarding a crime they had not committed, "Our hands have not shed this blood, nor have our eyes seen it . . . and do lay innocent blood . . . to the charge of thy people Israel" (Deut. 21:7–8).

Disaster in the Making

These two Court decisions—*Roe v. Wade* and *Lawrence v. Texas*— are catastrophic symbols of what has been happening to the country at large. Much of the nation outside the government, and especially all that pertains to the elite or the establishment, has been or has recently become in essence anti-Christian, anti-Jewish, anti-natural law, and implicitly or explicitly pagan. All of the nation's great secular universities, private and public, have turned pagan, with the exception of occasional faculty members, department heads, and other officials who have remained true to Christianity or observant Judaism. Even some confessionally bound universities, such as Baylor in Texas, are struggling to resist the trend. A few religiously affiliated colleges have remained loyal to their religious foundations. An even smaller number, such as Hillsdale College in Michigan, although not religiously affiliated, have managed to ignore the pressure to impose a totally naturalistic worldview on their students.

Many churches have fallen far away from the faith of their founders, as most recently and spectacularly the Episcopal Church has done by appointing an actively homosexual bishop. Indeed, we shall see that several churches have slowly accepted beliefs and patterns of conduct that radically deny their heritage, although seldom do they do so explicitly.

All this in itself is not yet a disaster, because as many rightly point out, there are many vestiges of authentic Christianity still to be found in our nation. But it would be a disaster for Christians and other God-fearers not to recognize that we've reached a turning point in our cultural history, and to go on dreaming that we can gradually change this formerly more-or-less Christian country for the better.

Those of us who are Christians and take our commitment seriously are slow to recognize it, but ultimately it will be easier for Christians to live in a country that we know is pagan than to live in one that we think is still sufficiently Christian to listen to us and to change in accordance with Christian values.

("The Christian View of America: Two Views," by Leith Anderson and Harold O. J. Brown was first published in Christianity Today, *August 2004, Page 38.)*

■ Open Up

Select one of these activities to launch your discussion time.

Option 1

Discuss these icebreaker questions:

• What adjectives would you use to describe America today? Brainstorm ten to twenty adjectives as a group.

• Step into the shoes of someone living in another country with a culture very different than our own, such as a person who grew up under Islamic law in the Middle East or a Chinese citizen who's always lived under communism. How would someone like this describe America? What adjectives might they use?

• Do you think the word "Christian" should be used to describe America? Why or why not?

Option 2

Get out some coins and bills and examine them closely, passing them around the group. Which of the faces, images, and words point toward God, Christianity, or Christian values? Share your observations. (Be sure all the money is returned to its owners!)

Brainstorm together other important American symbols, historical accounts, or documents that are connected with Christianity in some way.

Now talk about these questions:

- Our currency reads: "In God We Trust." Is this statement accurate? Do you think it should be on our currency? Why or why not?

- Do you think these allusions to Christianity from American history still have their place in today's America? Why or why not?

■ The Issue

Christians in America often debate how strong our nation's faith is. Evidences of sin abound, and some strains of sin run so deeply through our culture and government that you might conclude, along with Harold O. J. Brown, that America has become a pagan nation. Yet, as Leith Anderson notes, we also see enough evidences of genuine Christian faith that we should be encouraged.

- On balance, which of the following two statements do you think most accurately describes the spiritual condition of our country? Why? (No fence sitters!)

"It would be a disaster for Christians . . . to go on dreaming that we can gradually change this formerly more-or-less Christian country for the better."

—Harold O. J. Brown

"Christians are living holy lives that are having an enormous impact within our society."

—Leith Anderson

■ Reflect

Take a moment to read **Deuteronomy 21:1–9; Isaiah 8:11–22;** and **Matthew 13:24–30, 36–43** on your own. Write a few notes and observations about the passages: What do you see as the main ideas of each passage? What insights do they provide? What questions do they raise for you as you consider this issue?

■ Let's Explore

Both viewpoints—the "prophetic voice" (speaking against national sins) and the "Christian influencer" (seeking to make a difference within society)—find their basis in Scripture.

In his article, Harold O. J. Brown points to two pivotal Supreme Court rulings that he says effectively made the U.S. a pagan nation: *Roe v. Wade* and *Lawrence v. Texas*. Brown points to *Roe v. Wade* as "a clear repudiation of the biblical Judeo-Christian teaching that each human is made in the image of God," and to *Lawrence v. Texas* because in permitting sodomy, it repudiated "historic Christianity, the Bible, the Torah, and the principles of natural law that guided us so long."

- Do you see Brown's point? Do you think he overstates the situation? Would you add other evidences to bolster his argument?

- Leith Anderson points to many encouraging evidences of Christianity's influence in American society. What other examples would you add that are heartening to you?

Near the end of his article, Anderson includes a fascinating quote by Justin Webb, an atheist and a BBC correspondent, in which he describes average Americans as sharing "an uncomplicated faith."

- Read Webb's full quote from Anderson's article aloud in your group. What do you think of it? Do you think Webb's outsider perspective is an accurate reflection of America as you've personally experienced it? Why or why not?

The Bible sheds light on both Brown's and Anderson's perspectives. The prophets, for example, were often called by God to point out the deadly consequences of a nation's sin. But the gospel, as it is articulated throughout the Bible, reminds believers that we can make a difference in the culture in which we live.

- Which biblical example best reflects the mind-set you most often have toward our country? Do you tend to view our society through the eyes of a prophet, being saddened or angered by trends of godlessness and speaking out strongly against them? Or do you tend more toward the mind-set of a Christian influencer, focusing on the positive impact Christians are having on society and seeking to make a difference yourself?

When we find ourselves implicated in the wicked deeds of our society, we should seek God's atoning mercy.

Read Jesus's parable about the wheat and weeds in **Matthew 13:24–30** and his explanation in **verses 36–43**.

- When have you felt this way personally—like you were alone as a follower of Jesus, surrounded by those who belong to the Evil One? Share an example from your life.

- Ultimately, we do not believe the Lord is ever thwarted in his plans by Satan, so what possible benefit might our Sovereign Lord have in mind for believers to grow in fields alongside Satan's weeds?

Read **Deuteronomy 21:1–9**, a passage mentioned by Harold O. J. Brown.

- How would Brown suggest that we appropriate the truth of this somewhat obscure Old Testament law (especially vv. 7–8)?

- In what ways can we apply this text in forming our response to the sin in our country? In what ways can we pray that God will apply the atoning benefits of Christ's death to the sins of our nation?

This is not an easy question to answer, but this text does seem to carry the idea that God's people can be atoned for by Christ when we are unavoidably tied to the wickedness of our culture. It does not offer atonement for those who do not throw themselves on the mercy of God through repentance.

We, as God's people, maintain our unique perspective on the sinful society around us by taking advantage of our unique spiritual privileges.

Turn to Isaiah 8:11–22. God tells Isaiah how to keep his spiritual moorings in a society that gives God lip service but is determined to ignore both God's warnings and blessings. The tone is set in verse 11: "For the LORD spoke thus to me with a strong hand, and instructed me that I should not walk in the way of this poeple."

That is our challenge—not following the way of this people. Read together verses 11–13.

- The people around Isaiah feared two enemies to their north, even after God told them those enemies would prove to be no threat (Isa. 7:4–9). What are some of the fears of our society? Should we also have those fears? Why or why not?

Isaiah 8:13 points to fear of the Lord as an antidote to the fears of those around us. God's holiness is the measure of all that matters. The sovereign God decides what will happen according to his absolute sense of justice, his fiery righteousness, and his flaming truth. The future will not be decided by our political leaders or by international terrorists. The future will be decided by the Holy One! And what the Holy One decides about the future depends on how people respond to God's holy standards.

Read verses 14–15. In the passages before this, Isaiah has mentioned three times that God will send one called Immanuel, "God with us" (7:14; 8:8, 10). Immediately after this passage, he points clearly to Jesus Christ—9:1–7. That is whom he means here in verse 14 when he says, "he will be a sanctuary."

- How is Jesus Christ our sanctuary? How do you hide in him when circumstances in our country are frightening?

Read verses **16–22.**

- Isaiah storms over how people in his day would listen to the dead rather than listen to the living God, yet when life falls apart, they curse God. Where do people in our day turn for counsel?

Scripture grounds us in the truth and reminds us of the rich benefits of grace and righteousness. Through that grounding in truth, we ourselves become living "Scriptures" to the world around us, which will not likely listen to God any other way. Look again at verse **18.**

- How can we have this same kind of effect in our society? Share specific things Christians can or should do in order to live as "proofs" of God's existence and character.

■ Going Forward

We've looked together at just a few Scripture passages that provide guidance about how we are to relate to and live in a pagan society.

- What are some other Scripture passages and biblical teachings you rely on to guide the way you live in and respond to a pagan society? Why are they important to you?

Christians are in the world but not of it. We should never feel at home in our society. We can relate to both the pessimism of Harold O. J. Brown's assessment of our society and Leith Anderson's hopefulness.

- What does Harold O. J. Brown have to say to you personally through his article? Do you take the moral implications of the Supreme Court's decisions as seriously as he? Is there anything you can do?

- Does it help you to see Leith Anderson's perspective on the effect of Christians in America? If so, how? If not, why not?

Break into pairs to discuss this final question:

• Consider your mission living as a Christian in America. How has God spoken to you through these articles and Scripture passages? In what ways do you feel God challenging you to more stridently take a stand against evil in our society? Or what is one specific way you feel prompted by God to strive to influence our country for Christ?

Pray in pairs, asking God to help your partner respond to God's leading with action.

■ Want to Explore More?

Recommended Resources

Want to explore this topic further? Here are some resources that will help.

Leadership That Works: Hope and Direction for Church and Parachurch Leaders in Today's Complex World, Leith Anderson (Bethany, 2002; ISBN 0764226266)

Our Character, Our Future, Alan L. Keyes (Zondervan, 1996; ISBN 0310208165)

Becoming a Contagious Christian, Bill Hybels (Zondervan, 1996; ISBN 0310210089)

Rumors of Another World: What on Earth Are We Missing? Philip Yancey (Zondervan, 2003; ISBN 0310252172)

The Sensate Culture: Western Civilization Between Chaos and Transformation, Harold O. J. Brown (Wipf & Stock Publishers, 2007; ISBN 1556351887)

Slouching Towards Gomorrah: Modern Liberalism and American Decline, Robert Bork (Regan Books, 2003; ISBN 0060573112)

■ Notes

Should they be separate for

the sake of the church?

 SCRIPTURE FOCUS

John 8:31–36; Acts 16:16–34

1 Corinthians 7:21–24

2 Corinthians 11:1–15

CHURCH AND STATE:

KEEP THEM SEPARATE

■

The simple phrase "separation of church and state" is enough to get some people riled up, especially when it's used to curtail religious expression. None of us wants the government interfering with our religious rights. And yet many seem to want the government to not only allow us to exercise those rights but to essentially endorse them—because we are, after all, "a Christian nation," or at least we should be.

In this study, we'll look at two articles that discuss some recent church-state controversies, such as the Pledge of Allegiance and disagreements about information taught in public schools. In "Uncle Sam Is Not Your Dad," Stephen L. Carter argues that, as believers, we should embrace the separation of church and state. In "The Pledge Controversy," John Perry examines issues of religious expression and freedom of conscience. This Bible study takes a closer look at Carter's and Perry's ideas, exploring both the challenges and benefits of the separation of church and state.

■ Before You Meet

Read "Uncle Sam Is Not Your Dad" by Stephen L. Carter and "The Pledge Controversy" by John Perry from *Christianity Today* magazine.

UNCLE SAM IS NOT YOUR DAD

The separation of church and state protects families too.

By Stephen L. Carter

In an earlier column, I promised to discuss why I believe children should generally be exempt from courses of instruction in the public schools when the parents find the material objectionable on religious grounds. This is a controversial claim, and few educators, and even fewer courts, are likely to buy it. But the rationale is simple: when the state forces children to learn material that the parents find religiously offensive, it is, in nearly all cases, violating the separation of church and state.

Yes, that's right: the separation of church and state. That hoary and much-overused American tradition that has become, unfortunately, a tool for restricting the freedom of religion needs at last to be returned to its roots—as a tool for restricting government interference with the freedom of religion.

Although the "separation" that everyone talks about is nowhere mentioned in the Constitution, the principle was widely understood well before the framing of the First Amendment. But the way it was understood is very different from the casual use one hears today.

The idea that church and state should be separated is firmly grounded in Protestant theology. But the splitting of these two great institutions was only that—a splitting of institutions. Both were expected to continue to live under the rule of the one God.

For example, when Puritan New England banned clergy from officiating at marriages, authorities were certainly not suggesting that marriage should no longer be governed by God's rules. Rather, the goal was to avoid church corruption. The Puritans were reacting to the Church of England's role in ceremonies they believed the Bible did not specifically entrust to the ministry.

And when Roger Williams penned what seems to be the earliest American use of the metaphor—the garden and the wilderness, separated by a high hedge wall—he had in mind a wall protecting the garden from the wilderness, not the other way around.

This distinction matters. The garden, for Williams, was the beautiful yet fragile spot where the people of God nurtured their faith. This is where they strengthened each other, deepened their understanding and their commitment, and trained the next generation of believers. The wilderness represented the world, whose power and temptations posed many a threat to the garden. The wall kept the wilderness out.

So understood, separationism returns to its origins, as a principle for keeping the church pure, not a tool for keeping religious voices out of public life. Most important, it is supposed to protect the garden from interference as its people do the work that faith requires of them. That is the understanding the Framers probably were trying to enshrine when they drafted the religion clause (there is one clause, not two) of the First Amendment.

How does this approach apply to public education? It means that the state cannot, through its compulsory attendance laws, undercut the work of the garden. One obvious way of undercutting this work would be organized classroom prayer: surely, if the wall of separation protects the garden, the state cannot prescribe for the young when or how they should pray.

But other courses of instruction also pose problems, for there are many gardens, not just one. Some parents believe, for example, that classroom instruction in certain aspects of the theory of evolution interferes with their ability to nurture in their children a proper respect for God's Word and creation. Others fear that the particular way the schools teach tolerance will make it that much harder to instruct their children in the firm and clear moral rules they believe God commands. Except for instruction in what is held essential to American life—and this category should be small—the parental prerogative should be absolute. The First Amendment requires no less.

I do not mean this as an attack on the public schools, which are, I believe, a part of our nation's glory. Nor do I share the fears about a generation of illiterates if family freedom is so large. Parents as a group are neither idiots nor oppressors, and, if trusted to do so, will generally make wise decisions. But even when parents choose unwisely—selecting, for example, a church that teaches evil doctrines—the state may not interfere.

One might object that this proposal elevates the authority of the parents above the freedom of the child to choose. Precisely.

Stephen L. Carter is the William Nelson Cromwell Professor of Law at Yale University. He is the author of numerous books and is a regular columnist for Christianity Today.

("Uncle Sam Is Not Your Dad" was originally published in Christianity Today, *May 21, 2002, Vol. 46, No. 6, p. 68.)*

THE PLEDGE CONTROVERSY

Asking the wrong questions?

By John Perry

The federal court ruling prohibiting the Pledge of Allegiance from public schools came as a shock to many, but probably not to anyone familiar with the pledge's history. When it comes to the pledge in civic and religious life, the unexpected seems to be the norm. After all, this ruling comes mere months after the Pennsylvania House of Representatives passed a bill *requiring* all schools, public and private, to offer the pledge in every classroom on every day. Now, in a case unrelated to the Pennsylvania bill, we are told just the opposite: the pledge may *never* be recited in any classroom on any day. Such controversy is nothing new to the Pledge of Allegiance.

The pledge was written in 1892, and shortly thereafter dozens of school districts made its recitation mandatory. The first school children to refuse were Mennonites concerned that the pledge implied a military commitment. At that time, the pledge was part of a "flag salute ceremony" in which students raised their right arms toward the flag while reciting the words—the salute only reinforced Mennonite suspicions of military implications.

In the 1930s, Jehovah's Witnesses began to refuse the pledge as well as an act of solidarity with Witnesses in Germany facing Nazi persecution. How could American Witnesses salute a national flag when fellow believers were being sent to concentration camps for refusing much the same thing? The ACLU filed suit on behalf of Witness children who had been suspended for pledge refusal. In *Minersville School District v. Gobitis* (1940), the Supreme Court found mandatory pledges constitutional, resulting in an outbreak of violence against Witnesses. As a result of this violence, but also because forcing children to pledge looked a little too fascist for the times, the Court reversed itself three years later in *West Virginia State Board of Education v. Barnette*. Pledging has been optional ever since.

Using the pledge to distinguish America from its European enemies turns out to be a recurring theme. Hence in 1942 Congress noticed the disturbing similarity of the raised-arm salute to the stiff-arm Nazi salute and implemented the hand-over-heart posture. In 1954, Congress added the words "under God" to the pledge to distinguish America from the "godless" Soviet Union. It is this most recent modification that led to the controversial ban by the Ninth Circuit court.

What makes this case unlike past pledge controversies is that the plaintiff objects to his daughter even *hearing* the pledge. Hearing the reference to God is coercive, so the argument goes, and amounts to an established religion—the religion of monotheism, according to the court. This general type of argument is not altogether new. In a 1989 case involving a nativity scene and menorah on government property, the Supreme Court disagreed with the lower courts (who disagreed with each other) by prohibiting the nativity scene and permitting the less prominent menorah. As last week's decision found *hearing* coercive, the 1989 decision found *seeing* coercive.

Conservatives maintain that this latest ruling is a perversion of what the nation's founders intended. Liberals either agree with the conservatives, do not want to talk about it, or believe the decision *is* faithful to the founders. Yet surely the answer is not so simple when one branch of government demands pledge recitation, another branch prohibits it, and the highest court allows Hanukkah, but not Christmas, decorations. We must at least raise the possibility that neither conservatives nor liberals seem willing to consider: might all these disagreements and the accompanying court reversals be exactly what we should have expected the American system to produce?

Granted, James Madison could not have predicted this precise outcome, but might not his assumptions have made something like this inevitable? According to Madison, protections such as the First Amendment exist so that people are able to "pay homage" to the "Creator" freely, according to the "dictates of their conscience." The problem with Madison's reasoning, and the point at which it touches on the pledge controversy, is that it accepts the Enlightenment assumption that a conscience can actually and completely be "free." Under such an assumption it becomes increasingly difficult to avoid infringing on the dictates of everyone else's conscience.

Today, as such assumptions are called into question, it is no wonder that courts find themselves confused. Is a conscience free if it has seen Jesus in a manger at City Hall? Exactly how big can the Christ child be before my conscience has been coerced by seeing him sleep softly on public property? More to the point, can I hear my teacher say the words "under God" and still be sufficiently free to pay homage to God (or no god) according to *my own* conscience? At least within the Ninth Circuit, I cannot. But the conclusion to draw is neither that the decision is a perversion of the Constitution nor that it is good constitutional law. Rather, the presumption of a truly free conscience reflects an essential incoherence in the American understanding of church and state.

Legal scholars expect this ruling to be overturned either by the Supreme Court or, to save itself the indignity of such a reversal, by the

Ninth Circuit itself. But from a larger perspective, the outcome of this particular case is irrelevant. Is it coercive to merely hear the pledge? These judges say yes, others will say no. What no one questions is whether this is the right question to be asking—regardless of whether one is seeking to protect the state from the church or the church from the state. Perhaps in coming years, as the assumptions upon which Madison relied continue to give way, we will better understand what question we should be asking, and of whom we should ask it.

John Perry is a Ph.D. student in Christian Ethics at the University of Notre Dame.

("The Pledge Controversy" was first published in Christianity Today's *Books and Culture Corner Column, posted online July 8, 2002.)*

■ Open Up

Select one of these activities to launch your discussion time.

Option 1

Discuss one of these icebreaker questions:

- When you hear the phrase "separation of church and state," is your gut reaction negative, positive, or neutral? Why?

- Have you ever found yourself in the middle of a church/state conflict? Describe your situation and tell how it was resolved.

Option 2

Work together as a group to use LEGOs or children's wooden blocks to create two structures: one representing "the church" and one representing "the state." Also build a wall between the two structures. As you build, talk about the separation of church and state. Discuss these questions:

- What are some of the areas of politics, culture, or everyday life in which there's a "wall" dividing church and state?

- Do you generally view the separation of church and state positively or negatively?

Use your church/state structure as a visual symbol to spur discussion throughout the rest of the study.

■ The Issue

There are several issues and policies that have drawn fire in recent years and spurred debate about the separation of church and state, including:

— Controversies about public school curriculum (creation/evolution, sexual education, and so on)

— The Ten Commandments in courthouses or other public buildings

— Restricted political speech in churches

— The Pledge of Allegiance in public schools

— Federal funding for faith-based charities

— Allusion to monotheism on coins or other official state symbols

— Sectarian (Christian) prayers opening government meetings

— Controversies about tax exemptions for churches (including pastoral housing)

— Vouchers or other avenues of funding for private, religious schools

— Government interference in ministry organizations' hiring and firing practices

— Student-led prayer in public school functions like graduation ceremonies and football games

— Discuss a few of the issues mentioned above (or other church/state controversies that come to mind for you). What's your opinion about our country's current governmental or judicial policies on these issues? Explain.

The 2002 Ninth Circuit Court of Appeals' declaration that the Pledge of Allegiance was unconstitutional due to the "under God" phrase was not popular with the American people. In a *Newsweek* poll, an overwhelming 87 percent of respondents supported keeping "under God" in the pledge. Two months after the court's decision, in response to public outcry, the House of Representatives voted nearly unanimously to keep "one nation under God" as the official wording of the Pledge of Allegiance. *Newsweek* also reported that "84 percent [of Americans] think that references to God are acceptable in schools, government buildings, and other public settings." And in 2004, the Supreme Court dismissed the case challenging "under God" in the Pledge. Their decision, however, hung on a technicality—the Court did not directly address the broader questions about separation of church and state in their decision.

- Do you think references to God should be in public settings, on national symbols, or spoken as part of official government meetings? What about more specific references to Jesus? Explain.

- In his article, John Perry asserts that we may not be asking the right question, such as whether hearing the pledge—on account of the "under God" phrase—is a coercive and unconstitutional establishment of religion. But he does not tell us what he thinks the right question is. What do you think the right question is in this controversy?

■ Reflect

Take a moment to read **John 8:31–36; Acts 16:16–34; 1 Corinthians 7:21–24; and 2 Corinthians 11:1–15** on your own. Jot down some notes about the key ideas you observe. What are the major themes of these passages? What questions do these passages raise for you?

■ Let's Explore

We should strive to keep the church free from undue influence by the state.

Many today think of the separation of church and state in terms of keeping the influence of religion out of the realm of the state. But Stephen L. Carter points out that the original intent of this concept was just the opposite: to keep the influence of the state out of the realm of the church. He refers to Roger Williams' metaphor of the garden and the wilderness, saying "he had in mind a wall protecting the garden from the wilderness, not the other way around." Carter goes on to conclude that, "So understood, separationism returns to its origins, as a principle for keeping the church pure, not a tool for keeping religious voices out of public life."

- Why is it important to keep the church free from the state? What are the dangers of the state getting involved in the affairs of the church?

- What are some examples from history (or recent times) that reveal the danger of the state leading or influencing the church?

In **Ephesians 4:15–16**, Paul writes, "but, speaking the truth in love, may grow up in all things into Him who is the head—Christ—from whom the whole body, joined and knit together by what every joint supplies, according to the effective working by which every part does its share, causes growth of the body for the edifying of itself in love."

Christ *alone* is the head of the church—not the state, nor any human leader for that matter. In 2 Corinthians, Paul writes to correct the church in Corinth who had been swayed by human leaders preaching a distortion of the gospel and leading the church astray. Paul's message about the purity of the church—and the importance of protecting the church from corruption and ungodly leadership—can inform our understanding of our responsibility toward the church today.

Read **2 Corinthians 11:1–15.**

• How must we protect the church and keep it "pure" today? What boundaries should we maintain between the church and the state in order to protect the church from corruption of times past? Share specific examples.

Pastor Dietrich Bonhoeffer understood the danger of a commingling of the church and state in a way we don't today. He lived under the Nazi regime and strongly resisted their efforts to control the church. Bonhoeffer was eventually imprisoned and hanged for his part in a plot to assassinate Hitler.

While living under Nazi rule, Bonhoeffer sketched out his views on the way the church should relate to the state and the rights the church should expect from the state. He wrote:

[The Church] calls upon the persons who exercise government to believe in Christ for the sake of their own salvation. . . . Her aim is not that the government should pursue a Christian policy, enact Christian laws, etc., but that it should be true government in accordance with its own special task. . . . For the sake of their common Master, the Church claims to be listened to by the government; she claims protection for the public proclamation against violence and blasphemy; she claims protection for the institution of the Church against arbitrary interference, and she claims protection for the Christian life in obedience to Jesus Christ.

• What stands out to you most from Bonhoeffer's thoughts? How do his ideas impact the way you view the separation of church and state?

Policies based on the separation of church and state should not limit our free expression of faith in Christ.

The separation of church and state hinges on the establishment clause of the constitution which says:

Congress shall make no law respecting an establishment of religion, or prohibiting the free exercise thereof; or abridging the freedom of speech, or of the press; or the right of the people peaceably to assemble, and to petition the Government for a redress of grievances.

—First Amendment of the U.S. Constitution

• Taken at face value, what do you think this clause means? What doesn't it mean? What do you think motivated the early leaders of our country to include this amendment?

In recent times, controversies over the separation of church and state seem to have resulted in limiting religious expression rather than promoting religious freedom.

- What's been your experience? What are examples from current events in which the separation doctrine has served to remove God or expressions of faith from the public square?

The New Testament contains several examples of Christians being punished by the state for their bold declaration of the gospel. Read one such account found in **Acts 16:16–34.**

In some parts of the world today, Christians face this same threat: imprisonment by the state—or worse—for their expression of faith. There may be times when we, too, face social or even legal persecution for our expression of faith. Despite that persecution, we can follow the example of Paul and Silas—and indeed countless Christians jailed around the world today—who continued to proclaim the truth.

- Have you ever felt that your right to religious expression was being limited by laws or government policies? How about by social pressures? How did you respond? Share your experience.

Christian activist Jim Wallis once said, "I think it's very important that we affirm the separation of church and state. That doesn't mean the segregation of moral values from public life. But also, it doesn't banish religious language from the public square as long as we are respectful of diversity and pluralism and democracy."[1]

• How can we be bold and free in our expression of faith while also being respectful of the views of others who don't share our religious convictions? Give an example of what this might look like.

Ultimately our freedom does not depend on our social or political status or on legislative protection. Our freedom is found in our relationship with Christ.

Read 1 Corinthians 7:21–24.

People come to a saving knowledge and experience of Jesus in many different circumstances and stations in life. In Paul's own time there were "free people" who came to Christ; there were also "slaves" who came to Christ. Some were citizens of the Roman Empire; others were not.

Today, something similar could be said: some believers are employees; some are employers. Some are citizens in the countries in which they live; some are resident aliens. Furthermore, some live in countries with relative political and religious freedom; some live in countries that are quite repressive of religion and other basic human rights. Paul here seems to be saying, however, that our freedom doesn't depend on our social or religious status. Our true freedom depends on our relationship with Christ. He is the one who has bought our freedom with a price; through his atonement, we have experienced freedom from spiritual bondage and darkness, no matter what our social or political circumstances may be.

- In what ways are you a free person? In what ways are you not free?

- Think about our political, social, and religious freedoms in this land. Do they make a difference to your spiritual freedom and your relationship with Christ?

Freedom for many people means the absence of external controls—the freedom to do as one pleases. No one can tell them differently—not God, church, religion, school, parents, or state. The problem with this sense of freedom is that, ultimately, it becomes self-defeating: when we just give in to our own passions and impulses, doing whatever we please, we eventually become slaves to them. Not to mention that we're limited by other people's different expressions of freedom.

Read **John 8:31–36.** Jesus's listeners here had another notion: they thought they were free because they were descendants of Abraham. They remembered that it was God who had freed their ancestors from slavery in Egypt; since they were no longer to be slaves to despots like Pharaoh—or each other—didn't that make them free people?

Jesus had to set Abraham's descendants straight on two counts: truth comes before freedom, and freedom is essentially freedom from the guilt and compulsion of sin—not from ever sinning again. In other words: know Jesus—that's the truth—and you will then find freedom, true freedom, freedom from bondage to sin.

• What exactly does it mean to you to be free from the bondage of sin?

• How do you desire to share that truth and freedom with others? How might God be calling you to express that freedom in Christ in a more public manner?

■ Going Forward

In his book *God's Name In Vain,* Stephen L. Carter writes about the relationship between faith and politics, saying:

> On one side are those who treat the merest scintilla of religion in our public and political life as an offense against the American idea. On the other are those who believe it to be the responsibility of the government to use its power to enforce as law the moral truths of their religion. The tension between these two wrong ideas is ruining our democracy, and threatens to ruin many of our religious traditions as well.

• How do you see these wrong ideas "ruining our democracy?" What are examples of ways these wrong ideas are negatively impacting the church?

• In your opinion, how should the church relate to the state—and vice versa?

Form pairs, then share with your partner one specific way you feel challenged to protect the church or to express your faith. Pray together about specific church/state controversies that are on your mind. Also spend time thanking God for the ultimate freedom you find in Christ.

■ Want to Explore More?

Recommended Resources

Want to explore this topic further? Here are some resources that will help.

Online

Links to Stephen L. Carter's Civil Reactions column in *Christianity Today* can be found at http://www.christianitytoday.com/ct/features/opinion/columns/stephencarter/

Books

Church, State and Public Justice: Five Views, P.C. Kemeny, ed. (InterVarsity Press, 2007; ISBN 083082796X)

Separation of Church and State, Philip Hamburger (Harvard University Press, 2004; ISBN 0674013743)

That Godless Court? Supreme Court Decisions on Church-State Relationships, Second Edition, Ronald B. Flowers (John Knox, 2005; ISBN 0664228917)

■ Notes

What are the
possibilities—and
dangers—involved as
Christians increase their
power and influence in
politics and popular culture?

SCRIPTURE FOCUS

Luke 20:20–26, 22:24–27

Philippians 2:5–11

SHOULD CHRISTIANS

HAVE POWER?

■

In a recent *Christianity Today* article, Andy Crouch quotes film industry veteran Barbara Nicolosi as saying, "Within five to ten years, we will see Christians in Hollywood with real power." A quick review of the prominent political leaders of our country reveal that in Washington, D.C., at least, many self-proclaimed Christians already *do* hold significant positions of power and influence. Is Nicolosi's statement cause for celebration—or should it make us tremble at the dangers of such power?

As Crouch notes in his article "Glittering Images," Christians have reason to be, at the least, ambivalent about this matter of acquiring worldly power. After all, Jesus walked this earth in extraordinary humility and taught that the path to greatness is through sacrificial service. This lesson will look to Scripture and the example of Christ for guidance on the issue of power.

■ Before You Meet

Read "Glittering Images" by Andy Crouch from *Christianity Today* magazine.

GLITTERING IMAGES

A profound Christian rethinking of power is overdue.

By Andy Crouch

Barbara Nicolosi believes in the future of Christians in Hollywood. A Catholic veteran of the film industry who founded the screenwriting program Act One, she speaks enthusiastically of the time when believers will be well-enough represented in the ranks of studio executives to influence which films and TV series get the green light. "Right now, there simply aren't enough talented Christians who have paid their dues," she told a group of cultural-creative types in a coffeehouse near Washington, D.C., last fall. "But within five to ten years, we will see Christians in Hollywood with real power."

A young man wearing a beret waved his hand. "When you say 'Christians with power,'" he said, "I get really nervous."

"Well, you're here in Washington," Nicolosi responded. "Does it bother you that Christians have political power?"

"Yes it does, actually!" he responded—and a dozen others nodded intently in agreement.

Strange. No one would have been in that room, after all, if they didn't care quite a bit about power. Nicolosi filled a room and held our attention not just because of what she knew—though her knowledge of popular film and television is encyclopedic—but also whom she knew. In the currency of Hollywood, first-name anecdotes about Barbara Hall, producer of the spiritually attuned *Joan of Arcadia*, or Mel Gibson, director of *The Passion of the Christ*, are as good as gold.

Just as strange was the fact that many people in that room now have, or will soon acquire, significant power of their own. They aren't in Washington by accident—they have pursued a path of education, training, and apprenticeship designed to give them access to culturally influential vocations and locations.

Indeed, fifty years of evangelical efforts to reverse fundamentalism's cultural withdrawal have borne fruit. Christian colleges and universities, along with the ministries that are thriving in the penumbra of secular institutions, have nurtured a generation that takes cultural engagement for granted. Fundamentalists asked, Should we watch movies?—and usually, wary of worldliness, answered no. Evangelicals asked, What kind of movies should we watch?—and usually, wary of irrelevance, answered anything without sex. But now believers are asking, What kind of movies should we make? That's a question about power.

As Nicolosi's audience made clear, even many Christians who are acquiring power are ambivalent about it. The fourth century historian Eusebius could celebrate the life of Constantine, the first Christian emperor, with a heroic biography, conveniently glossing over small matters like the emperor's post-conversion murder of his wife and firstborn son. But we are millennia away from the euphoria that accompanied that first Christian ascent to cultural dominance. And in a post-Christian world, dominance is hardly in the cards. To acquire cultural influence one must cultivate numerous allies, most of them indifferent to faith, not to mention genuflect before consumer desires.

So a profound Christian rethinking of power—its possibilities and dangers—is overdue. Nearly twenty years ago, writer Richard Foster put the issue in context in *Money, Sex, and Power*. Each of these things, he observed, is fundamental to life, potentially full of blessing, and also potentially deceptive. Today there are sermon series and ministries to help Christians be stewards of their money. Store shelves groan under the weight of Christian books on sex. But Christian reflection on power generally stops with business-friendly topics like "leadership." Cultural power often accrues less from leadership than from connections, talent, and fame—not to mention money and sex. (There's a reason that the top-grossing star of *What Women Want* was able to make a movie about the Passion.)

Indeed, Christians who want to think more deeply about these things might well go to Mel Gibson's movie, whose controversy-ridden existence indicates the extent, and the limits, of Christian cultural power today. The Passion of Christ, after all, reminds us of the many ways that power can go wrong—a nervous procurator with his garrison of occupying troops, a conniving royal family with paper-thin claims to legitimacy, religious leaders bent on preserving pious decorum amid precarious alliances.

At the center of it all we find a thirty-something man with considerable political savvy, a gifted storyteller with a keen eye for shrewd symbolic acts. Moreover, he has the divine power to multiply loaves of bread, heal the sick, and raise the dead. Yet his most decisive, powerful act is not an action at all, but a passion—suffering the brunt of power itself, grieving, forgiving, waiting. If Christians are sometimes called to acquire power, we should probably begin by watching our Lord abandon it.

Andy Crouch is editor of the *Christian Vision Project* (www.christianvisionproject. com).

("Glittering Images" was first published in *Christianity Today*, February 2004, Page 78.)

■ Open Up

Select one of these activities to launch your discussion time.

Option 1

Discuss one of these icebreaker questions:

- Complete this sentence, any way you'd like: "I wish I had the power to . . ."

- Imagine you were offered the job of president of the United States. Would you want the job? Explain your rationale.

- First Baron Acton John Emerich Edward Dalberg, in 1887, said, "Power tends to corrupt, and absolute power corrupts absolutely. Great men are almost always bad men." Do you agree with this observation? Do you think it is always true, generally true, or just occasionally true? Why?

Option 2

Everyone should bring to the study several recent newspapers and some news and entertainment magazines. Take a few minutes to page through the magazines and newspapers, cutting out pictures or names of those you'd consider some of the most powerful people in the world today. When your group has a good-sized pile, spread out all the names and images, then discuss this question as a group:

- Are there any notable powerful people missing from our collection? Who are they?

On scrap paper, write down their names (or if you're up for some fun, quickly doodle their images) and add them to the collection. Now, privately create a top ten list from the names and faces your group has collected. Who do you think are the ten most powerful people in our world today? Be sure to rank your list in order, with one as the most powerful.

After a moment, compare your top ten lists within the group, then try to come to a consensus on the top five. Use the paper names and faces to create a visual top five list for your group. When you're done, discuss these questions:

- How have these people used their power to influence the world? Positively or negatively? Share examples.

- How do you think wielding such power has affected these people? Do you think it has corrupted them in some way? Explain.

■ The Issue

Political leaders like Condoleeza Rice, George W. Bush, Bill and Hillary Clinton, Colin Powell, and Barack Obama, and entertainers like Jessica Simpson, Mel Gibson, Bono, and Miley Cyrus are highly paid, newsworthy people. They are prominent in a variety of ways, and they have one thing in common: they have all claimed to be Christians. Many believers feel proud when Christians achieve such fame and influence. Yet, ought we to be uneasy that there are some who mix discipleship and power so easily? As the young man is quoted in Andy Crouch's article, "When you say 'Christians in power,' I get really nervous."

- How have these famous people influenced the wider culture for Christianity? Name others who combine Christianity with worldly power and prestige.

Andy Crouch reminds us there was a day when Christians avoided contact with the world and withdrew from the culture. But over the past fifty years, evangelicals have succeeded in areas like politics and popular culture that once were considered off-limits.

- Have evangelical Christians too whole-heartedly entered into the culture? Should we be "really nervous" about further acquirement of power? Explain.

■ Reflect

Take a moment to read **Luke 20:20–26, 22:24–27** and **Philippians 2:5–11** on your own. Jot down a few notes and observations about the passages: What insights do these passages give you about power? Which images, words, or phrases stand out to you the most? What questions do you have about these passages?

■ Let's Explore

Jesus called his followers to service rather than dominance.

- When you think of Jesus, do you think of him as a powerful figure? Give examples of how Jesus demonstrated power or powerlessness.

Read **Philippians 2:5–11**. Scholars believe this passage may have been an early Christian hymn that Paul quoted. It speaks of the self-emptying of Christ who, though he was "in the form of God," did not act like we expect God to act. Rather, he took "the form of a servant" and "humbled himself." Scholars sometimes refer to this passage as the "kenosis hymn," from the Greek word that means "emptying." This humbling of himself was a major reason many did not recognize Jesus as the long-awaited Messiah.

- Have you ever found it challenging to serve the God who, as the Suffering Servant, seemed less than powerful? What are some ways, in Scripture or in your personal experience, that God did not seem to act like an all-powerful deity?

Jesus said much to his followers about what they were to do when they were persecuted, unjustly condemned, and forced to suffer for his sake. But he gave no specific instructions about how to run a bank, or operate a newspaper, or rule over a city.

Andy Crouch cites Constantine as an example of how the church may have sold out when it was adopted as a part of the state. Although imperial persecution of the church ceased, the church was tied to the mechanism of state power. Constantine became a friend of the church, but it was a friendship that demanded much of the church.

- In your view, does Jesus expect his followers to be permanently in positions of powerlessness, marginalization, and humility? Why or why not?

- Can Christians serve and do good in the world by making allies with non-Christians, or does that always result in ungodly compromise? Is this as true in the arena of politics as it may be in other arenas such as the business world or entertainment? Give some examples.

Christians ought to be uneasy about making alliances with the means and goals of this culture.

Andy Crouch questions whether evangelical Christians have too easily, or too uncritically, bought into many of this culture's definitions of power. With the example of Constantine, he reminds us that to get influence and power in the world, we sometimes endanger the truth of the gospel.

At the beginning of his ministry (Luke 4:1–13), Jesus was tempted by Satan in the wilderness. Satan offered Jesus power to do good (turn stones to bread), power to accomplish great spiritual feats (throw himself down from the temple tower), and political power (authority over all the kingdoms of the world). Jesus began his ministry by rejecting these tempting invitations. He resisted the attempts of his followers to make him a king and instead knelt down with basin and towel and washed their feet before he went to die on a cross.

- Are Christians deluding themselves when they think they can exercise worldly power without damaging their faithfulness to Christ? Why or why not?

- Crouch says there are many ways our exercise of power can go wrong. In what ways can people in power get seduced and used by the very power they think they are using for good?

- Have you seen a Christian in power resist this temptation and maintain Christian values within his or her role? Share an example.

Read **Luke 22:24–27**. Here, at the Last Supper, Jesus shared with his disciples a picture of the peculiar nature of Christian discipleship. Jesus is waiting on the table, serving his followers, and what are his followers doing? They are debating who is greatest in the kingdom of God!

Jesus reminds them that he is one who serves, and they should follow his example.

- How does Luke 22:24–27 apply to leaders? Name specific ways leaders, particularly those in politics, can practice this kind of servanthood. (If you've observed servant leadership in Christian political leaders, share some specific examples.)

In response to a text like **Luke 22:24–27**, some Christians use this reasoning: Christians in the first century were persecuted and despised by the imperial authorities. Today we are fortunate to live in a democratic country where we have freedom of religion. Therefore, if we have the opportunity to use positions of power to accomplish good for our world, then we ought to do so.

- Does living in a country with religious freedom and democratic government make Christians less likely to abuse power? Why or why not?

Christians need to exercise careful, prayerful use of power and remain wary of its ambiguities and challenges.

- Do you generally tend to seek after positions of leadership, influence, and power? Or do you usually shun or avoid those positions? How is your answer a reflection of your personality? How is it a reflection of your views on the dilemma we face as Christians when it comes to the issue of power?

Read **Luke 20:20–26.** In an attempt to entrap Jesus, his critics asked him if they ought to honor Caesar by paying taxes. Jesus famously replied, "Give to Caesar the things that are Caesar's, and give to God the things that are God's."

- Even though Jesus was talking about money, think of it in the context of today's society. Generally speaking, what do you view as "Caesar's"? What do you think of as God's?

When William H. Willimon, a professor at Duke University, taught this passage to a group of students, one person said, "But Jesus doesn't tell us what belongs to Caesar and what belongs to God." Willimon and the students shared their perplexity at the inexactitude of Jesus's answer. Then one of the students said, "Maybe the vagueness of the answer means that when it comes to relations between Christians and the government, we are supposed to be permanently uneasy."

Perhaps that is a good, biblical response to the dilemma of Christians in power. After all, it is impossible for anyone to avoid all means of power: we all have some amount of money, things, and influence.

- In light of the biblical material on power and its dangers, can a strong case be made for all Christians to shun power? Explain.

■ Going Forward

Break into pairs to discuss these questions:

- Give a specific example of a time when you felt a dilemma between power and your Christian faith. How did you handle that situation? Do you wish you had handled it differently? If so, how?

- If your best friend was in a powerful position—a politician or celebrity, for example—how would you advise that person to use that power well? How would you advise that person to avoid the "corrupting" influences of power? Be specific.

Write down several specific items of advice you and your partner discussed, then gather back together as a group to discuss this final question:

- Share your words of advice about handling power with the rest of the group. Now consider this: how do these words of advice apply to you and the situations in which you lead, influence others, or possess power? Share your personal response to these words of advice.

Close with prayer, asking for Christ's guidance in our daily dilemmas and struggles to be Christians in a sometimes conflicted and demanding world. If God brings to mind specific Christians in positions of power, pray for them by name, asking God to strengthen and encourage them as they strive to honor him.

■ Want to Explore More?

Recommended Resources

Want to explore this topic further? Here are some resources that will help.

The Challenge of the Disciplined Life: Christian Reflection on Money, Sex, and Power, Richard J. Foster (Harper SanFrancisco, 1989; ISBN 0060628286)

Church on Sunday, Work on Monday: The Challenge of Fusing Christian Values with Business Life, Laura Nash, Ken Blanchard, and Scotty McLennan (Jossey-Bass, 2001; ISBN 0787956988)

Resident Aliens: Life in the Christian Colony, William H. Willimon and Stanley M. Hauerwas (Abingdon Press, 1989; ISBN 0687361591)

Selling Out the Church: The Dangers of Church Marketing, Philip D. Kenneson and James L. Street (Wipf & Stock Publishers, 2003; ISBN 159244296X)

■ Notes

How much hope should

Christians place in political

solutions to our problems?

Isaiah 40:12–31, 46:9–11

Romans 6:1–14, 12:1–2

RELYING ON

GOVERNMENT . . . OR GOD?

■

It doesn't take longer than a few seconds for the average person to begin rattling off answers to the question, "How has the government let you down?" From potholes in the highway to empty political promises to images of seemingly preventable tragedies—such as the 9/11 attacks—examples of the failures of government are not hard to come by. But despite our readiness to complain, we continue to place great hope in the government and to rely on it to keep our lives safe and sound. Certainly the government does play an important and positive role in our lives and global community, but are our expectations unrealistic? Too high? Perhaps even *wrong*?

In "Your Government Failed You," Bob Wenz examines some of the expectations he believes people wrongly place on the government—namely the hope that the government can protect us from all potential tragedies and attacks. To do so, Wenz points out, the government would need to be both omniscient and omnipotent.

In "Children of a Lesser Hope," David P. Gushee critiques a different sort of dependence on the government: Christians relying on politics and legislation to uphold moral standards and promote right living. "The New Testament writers show great confidence that the world is being transformed through the redemptive work of Jesus Christ," says David P. Gushee. "But they show no confidence whatsoever that the powers and principalities of this world serve as the agents of that global transformation." Yet many believers, it seems, persist in relying on government and political maneuvers to transform the morals of society.

This study will examine Wenz and Gushee's ideas as we look at the fine line between relying on the government and placing our hope in God.

■ Before You Meet

Read "Your Government Failed You" by Bob Wenz and "Children of a Lesser Hope" by David P. Gushee from *Christianity Today* magazine.

YOUR GOVERNMENT FAILED YOU

But then, we don't want an all-powerful government
any more than we want an all-powerful God.

By Bob Wenz

Last March former White House terrorism adviser Richard Clarke told the National Commission on Terrorist Attacks Upon the United States that the U.S. government "failed to prevent the tragedy of 9/11." He proceeded to apologize for that failure.

At the same hour that Clarke testified to the 9/11 Commission, the Supreme Court heard arguments in *Elk Grove Unified School District v. Newdow.* There Michael Newdow argued that the United States no longer should be acknowledged as "one nation under God." Those two hearings may at first glance seem unrelated. But there is an important link.

Of course the government failed to prevent the attack on the Twin Towers. But beyond that, the government also failed to prevent the Chicago Fire, the San Francisco Earthquake, the Johnstown Flood, the St. Valentine's Day Massacre, the stock-market crash of 1929, the Holocaust, the AIDS epidemic, the Oklahoma City bombing, the Columbine killings, Hurricane Whatshername, the Enron meltdown, and a long list of other tragedies and disasters, both natural and man-made.

Clarke seemed to presume that "your government" should somehow have been able to anticipate and prevent evil from happening—both the evil that we call *natural disasters*, and the evil that comes directly from the hearts and hands of evil people. It is a false premise. To presume the government's ability to prevent such a catastrophe is to assume that it possesses qualities and abilities that no person, let alone a government, can ever possess.

Omniscience and *omnipotence* are qualities that we ascribe only to God. Clarke fails to recognize the inherent limitations of government. The U.S. Constitution certainly envisions no omniscience or omnipotence for the federal government.

In fact, the Constitution sets comparatively modest, human-sized objectives for the government: "to form a more perfect union, establish justice, insure domestic tranquility, provide for the common defense, promote the general welfare, and secure the blessings of liberty to ourselves and our posterity." Those finite tasks are challenging enough. Providing for the "common defense" is a noble task for a government. Protecting every citizen from any kind of harm is quite another matter.

Pledging Allegiance

On the same day that we heard that our government had failed, Newdow argued before the U.S. Supreme Court that "under God" should be removed from the Pledge of Allegiance.

One cannot help being struck by the irony of these hearings taking place only hundreds of feet apart. At issue in both hearings was the same question: Are we "under God"?

Let us be careful here. If there is a Creator, then we are "under God" whether we acknowledge it in a pledge or not. If there is a Creator, then we are creatures. If there is a Creator, then he is the one who is omniscient and omnipotent, and not us.

Many Americans are "practical atheists" who have long since forsaken a Creator and a theistic worldview—and in the process have seemingly transferred onto the government the divine qualities of omniscience and omnipotence. For centuries people have tended to blame God for not preventing everything bad that happens. In fact, Freud (and others) posited that God is merely a human invention created to explain and possibly to blame for those phenomena that cannot otherwise be rationally explained. Many now blame the government because they presume it should possess the divine foreknowledge and requisite power to protect citizens from all harm.

Exactly how this transferal took place is a mystery, but it seems to reflect the erosion of the dominant theistic worldview and the growing acceptance of a naturalistic worldview. Perhaps it was Freud's influence. Perhaps the growing "victim mentality" in our culture (which some call "the Oprahfication of America") played a part.

Yet, all the interpreters and advocates of the secular worldview have only managed to marginalize what they consider the outmoded theistic worldview. They offer no new insights to explain the anomalies of life. In place of God, government—a most imposing institution that also seems bigger than life—has assumed the default position.

Most bad things happen in our world because humanity is inherently sinful. In some cases, that disposition spills over the moral dams and results in great and senseless acts of evil, be it individual (Timothy McVeigh or Columbine High School killers Eric Harris and Dylan Klebold) or collective (the Holocaust).

Of course, this view of human nature flies in the face of the romanticized evolutionary worldview of progressivism that humankind is basically good and getting better, only in need of more, better, and politically correct education. We ought to recall, however, that the U.S. Constitution purposefully delineated the separation of the branches of government, articulating the "balance of powers" based on the worldview that human nature is corrupt.

Happy Evil

The Creator (whom Jefferson cited in the Declaration of Independence) has "endowed us" with the right to pursue happiness. But that endowment to very evil people like Dylan Klebold or Timothy McVeigh can result in the evil pursuit of a perverted happiness. A chilling reminder of this is the videotape of Osama bin Laden celebrating the destruction of the World Trade Center.

Because our world has a significant number of evil people who pursue their happiness in this way, it is impossible to prevent them without being both omniscient and omnipotent. Government cannot anticipate and prevent every evil act hatched in the imaginations of evil people.

When seriously evil people succeed in their pursuit of happiness, many believers angrily ask: Why didn't God stop it? Why didn't God exercise his omniscience and omnipotence and prevent it from happening? In fact many have abandoned faith in God because they cannot find a satisfactory answer to this question.

Yet our omnipotent and omniscient Creator has decided not to directly restrain our evil tendencies. He does not systematically prevent those he endowed with the unalienable rights of life, liberty, and the pursuit of happiness from using those liberties to do evil. Likewise, he does not cause our computers to crash to keep us from filing false tax returns. He does not cause us to go blind to prevent us from viewing child pornography.

Somehow, though, when evil people shoot at students and teachers in Columbine High School, we expect God to turn bullets into marshmallows. We expect him to turn hijacked airliners away from tall buildings. (Curiously, the one plane that did not find its target on September 11 was diverted by a group of people—led by a Christian—who sought to prevent greater evil than that which they faced. Todd Beamer understood the biblical exhortation to "overcome evil with good.")

While God does not directly intervene to restrain our evil tendencies, he has ordained human government to function in that capacity to a limited degree—to punish evildoers. Hence it is not surprising that unbelievers (both philosophical atheists and practical atheists) now ask: why didn't the government stop it?

The irony, of course, is that many of those who want or expect the government to prevent evil strongly resist the government's growing need for knowledge and power to act effectively in protecting the American public.

"My government failed!" Of course my government failed. Americans, keenly focused on "life, liberty, and the pursuit of happiness," have made it clear they are unwilling to remove limits on the ability of government both to *know* and to *interfere* in that highly individualized pursuit. The Patriot Act has reminded us that the expectation of government to protect us quickly runs aground on the rocks of surveillance laws, privacy rights, and the overall "pursuit of happiness" Americans enjoy.

In essence, we don't want an omniscient and omnipotent government for the same reasons we reject the idea of a nation "under God." So we end up holding both at arm's length. We don't want an all-knowing and all-powerful entity in our lives—except, perhaps, when evil strikes us from abroad or disaster befalls us, and we need someone to blame.

Bob Wenz coaches churches and trains pastors through Renewing Total Worship Ministries. He is a board member of the National Association of Evangelicals and an adjunct faculty member at Kings College and Seminary and at Pikes Peak College.

("Your Government Failed You" was originally published in Christianity Today *February 2005, Vol. 49, No. 2.)*

CHILDREN OF A LESSER HOPE

What happens when we lose confidence in the church.

By David P. Gushee

I am a Christian ethicist, but there's something wrongheaded about much Christian social ethics. In graduate school, I learned to examine some social problem in detail, then bring Christian principles thoughtfully to bear on that problem. Curiously, this process most often results in statements about what *government*—not the church—should do about the particular problem.

Mainline Protestants have dominated the discipline of Christian social ethics from its beginning, but today it is conservative evangelical Christians who are most vocal and visible in telling government what it should and should not do. Sometimes this involves analysis. Often it merely involves raised voices.

Now certainly, the United States government should not be the primary audience for Christian ethics. Over the past forty years, ethicists beginning with John Howard Yoder and then Stanley Hauerwas have strongly objected to this development. There is something quite wrong, they say, when the intended audience for Christian moral reasoning is the secular world and the institutions that govern it.

This simply does not fit with the biblical witness, especially in the New Testament. The ethical exhortations offered there are articulated for followers of Jesus Christ by Jesus himself or by his apostles. New Testament moral teachers aim to instruct *Christians* in what manner of life is worthy of those whose identity is bound up with that of Christ. Think, for example, of Paul's great ethical exhortations in Romans. Having been chosen by God and baptized into Christ's death and resurrection, we are to offer ourselves as a living sacrifice, not conformed to the world, but transformed by the renewing of our minds.

The New Testament writers show great confidence that the world is being transformed through the redemptive work of Jesus Christ. But they show no confidence whatsoever that the powers and principalities of this world serve as the agents of that global transformation. No, the redemption of the world is God's activity, occurring in God's good time. It is an ongoing process in which the church is intimately involved, through faithful pursuit of its mission, but also, quite simply, through its quiet daily practice of God's will.

Generally speaking, American evangelicals have a poorly developed theology of the church. We also produce a variety of expressions of church life that do not emphasize rigorous moral commitment. Our pietistic individualism creates a "Jesus and me" ethos that often weakens any loyalty to the community of faith or any willingness to submit to a disciplined covenantal vision. *The church is where I go to get my spiritual needs met—you have no right to tell me what to do as I pursue that quest.*

The moral mediocrity of this kind of church can leave us hopeless about the church as the center of God's redemptive enterprise in the world. How can we truly believe that the world's transformation is happening right here, right among us, when we can't stop divorce in our midst, or abortion, or greed, or internal church conflicts?

Ironically, we turn to the state to enforce the values we can't seem to advance in our own churches. We're rightly concerned about our collapsing families, internet pornography, decadent movies and music, and the weakening of sexual morality. But we often can't seem to prevent the encroachment of these problems in our own Christian families and congregations. As if in response, we keep trying to change our nation's laws.

The Church's Message

Is there a direct correlation between our declining confidence in the church and our growing engagement with politics? The more we find it hopeless to think that we can actually create and sustain disciplined communities of faith, the more we spend our time on political activities. We may not be able to get self-identified Christians to obey the Word of God, but we might be able to leverage our political clout to elect "our people" to Congress.

Recently I was brought up short by reading about an Ohio pastor who was hoofing it through his neighborhood getting the work of the church done. No, he wasn't visiting the sick, preaching the gospel, or inviting people to church. He was registering voters. Call me old-fashioned, but somehow that doesn't seem quite right to me. I'm glad it's not how my own pastor invests his time.

It is election season, and we must remember that there are many good reasons to exercise our Christian citizenship with care. But the church's *message* is that *Jesus* saves.

David P. Gushee is Graves Professor of Moral Philosophy at Union University. His books include *Only Human: Christian Reflections on the Journey Toward Wholeness, Getting Marriage Right: Realistic Counsel for Saving and Strengthening Relationships,* and he is coauthor of *Kingdom Ethics: Following Jesus in Contemporary Context.*

("Children of a Lesser Hope" was originally published in Christianity Today, *November 2006.)*

■ Open Up

Select one of these activities to launch your discussion time.

Option 1

Discuss one of these icebreaker questions:

• Do you generally have a positive view or a negative view of the federal government? How about local government? Why?

• If you were running for president, what would be the main issues on your platform? In other words, what would you most want to change about our country or about the government?

- What about if you were running for local office, such as mayor or even governor? What local issues would you key in on as the most important for the government to address?

Option 2

Each person should grab a pen and a piece of notebook paper. When everyone is ready, take two minutes to individually brainstorm and write down as many answers as you can to the question below. Your goal is to think of and write down more answers than the others in the room; you can write short one- to three-word answers. The question is:

- What positive things does the government do that in some way affect your life?

When everyone is ready, begin writing. At the end of two minutes, take turns reading off the items from your list. When someone mentions an answer that you've also written, you all must cross that answer off your list. At the end, tally up your remaining unique answers, then see who's won.

Then discuss these questions:

- Did you find it challenging to think of positive things the government does for you? Why or why not?

- Do you generally think of the government in a positive or negative light? Why?

■ The Issue

In their articles, Bob Wenz and David P. Gushee zero in on two arenas in which many, they claim, wrongly rely on the government when they should be relying on God. Wenz highlights the commonly held notion that it is the government's job to protect us and keep us safe from danger and disaster. Gushee points to a subtler yet equally dangerous reliance on the government: Christians desiring that the government bring about moral change through legislation.

- When it comes to protection from danger or prevention of disasters, what do you think is reasonable to expect from the government? What is unreasonable? Give examples.

- In the area of morality, in what ways should we expect the government to uphold moral standards? What areas, do you think, may be outside the government's purview? Give examples.

■ Reflect

Take a moment to read **Isaiah 40:12–31, 46:9–11; Romans 6:1–14,** and 12:1–2 on your own. Jot down the words or phrases that seem most important to you. What are the key ideas in these passages? How do the passages compare or contrast with one another? What questions do they raise for you?

■ Let's Explore

God alone is all-powerful and all-knowing.

There's been much blame passed around for the 9/11 attacks. Perhaps some of that blame is deserved; after all, the government *did* fail to prevent that tragedy from occurring. In his article Wenz goes on to highlight a myriad of other horrific tragedies that also weren't prevented by the government, including "the Chicago Fire, the San Francisco Earthquake, the Johnstown Flood, the St. Valentine's Day Massacre, the stock-market crash of 1929, the Holocaust, the AIDS epidemic, the Oklahoma City bombing, the Columbine killings, Hurricane Whatshername, the Enron meltdown, and a long list of other tragedies and disasters, both natural and man-made."

• What other recent tragic events might you add to Wenz's list? How do you feel when you read a list like this? Why?

• Do you think the government could have prevented 9/11 or other recent tragedies? Why or why not?

Wenz refers to both human-caused events and natural disasters when he writes, "To presume the government's ability to prevent such a catastrophe is to assume that it possesses qualities and abilities that no person, let alone a government, can ever possess. *Omniscience* and *omnipotence* are qualities that we ascribe only to God."

The Bible describes God's omniscience (all-knowing nature) and his omnipotence (all-powerful nature) in a variety of passages. Read some of these descriptions in **Isaiah 40:12–31** and **46:9–11**. (You may also want to read Isaiah 45:21 and Hebrews 4:13.)

- What descriptions of God or aspects of his nature most stand out to you from these passages? Why?

For some, belief in God's omniscience and omnipotence is a source of great comfort during times of tragedy. Yet for others, this belief causes intense questioning. Wenz notes that after a horrific tragedy, many Christians wonder, "Why didn't God stop it? Why didn't God exercise his omniscience and omnipotence and prevent it from happening?" He goes on to say,

> Many have abandoned faith in God because they cannot find a satisfactory answer to this question. Yet our omnipotent and omniscient Creator has decided not to directly restrain our evil tendencies. He does not systematically prevent those he endowed with the unalienable rights of life, liberty, and the pursuit of happiness from using those liberties to do evil. Likewise, he does not cause our computers to crash to keep us from filing false tax returns. He does not cause us to go blind to prevent us from viewing child pornography. Somehow, though, when evil people shoot at students and teachers in Columbine High School, we expect God to turn bullets into marshmallows. We expect him to turn hijacked airliners away from tall buildings.

- How does your belief in God's omniscience and omnipotence square with the very real tragedy and evil of disastrous events? In your opinion, does Wenz's answer above address the issue satisfactorily? Why or why not?

No matter how much money we pour into Defense and Intelligence, the government will never have the power or knowledge to protect our country from every possible threat. And no matter how many geologists or meteorologists or engineers we put on the job, the government will never be able to protect our nation from the results of natural disasters. Ultimately, only God can know what is going to happen and can wield the power to allow it or prevent it; ultimately, our lives are in God's hands— not the government's.

God alone can change hearts and renew minds.

There are many ongoing controversies in our country about laws and court cases that attempt to "legislate morality," especially in areas such as homosexuality and marriage, profanity in the media, embryonic research, corporate finance, drug and alcohol use, and assisted suicide. Yet even aside from these controversies, many established and unquestioned laws *do* in fact legislate morality, such as laws forbidding assault, burglary, child pornography, and murder.

- Do you think laws that attempt to control morality assist in the transformation of behavior? Why or why not? Defend your view.

- Do you think Christians who put great effort into promoting and passing "moral" laws (like embryonic stem-cell research legislation, a federal marriage amendment, anti-abortion legislation, and so on) are doing God's work? Or are they wasting their time? Should their efforts be focused elsewhere? Explain.

Read **Romans 6:1–14** and **12:1–2**. The moral character of a nation must be rooted in the hearts and minds of its individual members. Through the redemptive work of Christ, we have the power to conform our thinking and behavior to God's will. Legislation may promote the outward appearance of obedience, but God alone can produce true moral change in the lives of individuals and nations.

The apostle Paul warned the Romans not to conform to this world. Gushee says, "The more we find it hopeless to think that we can actually create and sustain disciplined communities of faith, the more we spend our time on political activities."

- In what ways should a Christian act differently from the rest of the world? Do you agree with Gushee that many Christians today are hard to distinguish from the rest of the world? If yes, what accounts for the discrepancy between their statement of belief and their behavior?

- Do you think stronger moral legislation would improve the morality of the church? Would it improve the morality of the nation as a whole? Why or why not?

Gushee believes that American evangelicals struggle with moral mediocrity to the point that we are left feeling hopeless about the church as the center of God's redemptive work in the world. Gushee believes this feeling of hopelessness causes us to turn to the state to enforce values.

- Do you agree with Gushee? Why or why not? Share examples you've observed.

Gushee says, "The redemption of the world is God's activity, occurring in God's good time. It is an ongoing process in which the church is intimately involved, through faithful pursuit of its mission, but also, quite simply, through its quiet daily practice of God's will."

- Where should the emphasis on moral commitment begin? What role should the church have in helping define and shape the values and morals of our nation?

■ Going Forward

Discuss this question as a group:

• In light of all you've discussed, what conclusions have you drawn about the proper perspective a Christian should have on the government? To what degree—if at all—should we look to politics to prevent or solve our problems?

Form pairs and discuss these questions together:

Psalm 20:7 says, "Some trust in chariots, and some in horses; But we will remember the name of the LORD our God." A contemporary reading of the verse might go something like this: "Some trust in governments, presidents, laws, and armed forces—but we trust in the Lord our God."

• How fully do you rely on God and trust in him in your everyday life? Do you feel Psalm 20:7 speaks true when it comes to your own life? Explain.

Re-read Isaiah 40:28–31 with your partner.

• In light of all you've discussed, what does it mean to you to "trust the Lord" or "hope in the Lord" (NIV)? How do you feel challenged to more fully rely on him?

Take a moment on your own to re-write Psalm 20:7 in your own words. In the first part, list the people or institutions or things in which you may at times be tempted to place too much trust. Then, with resolution, write your commitment to trust fully in God alone.

Gather back together as a group and spend time praying. Focus your prayer time on praising God for his trustworthiness and committing to more fully rely on him rather than on human efforts or endeavors.

■ Want to Explore More?

Recommended Resources

Want to explore this topic further? Here are some resources that will help.

Christians and Politics Beyond the Culture Wars: An Agenda for Engagement, David P. Gushee (Baker, 2000; ISBN 0801022312)

Faith & Politics: What's a Christian to Do?, C. Welton Gaddy (Smyth & Holwys Publishing, Inc., 1996; ISBN 1573120464)

Jesus and Politics: Confronting the Powers, Alan Storkey (Baker, 2005; ISBN 0801027845)

There's More to Life Than Politics, William Murchison (Spence Publishing Company, 1998; ISBN 0965320839)

Bonus Small-Group Builder

from www.smallgroups.com

You can find more helpful insights for small group health at
www.smallgroups.com.

There's nothing like politics to bring an edge of heated debate to a group discussion. Well, maybe *religion* . . .

What is that old saying? "Don't talk about politics and religion . . ." Well, what about *both* . . . *together?* That's a scary thought!

As you go through this study on politics together in your small group, you're going to have some great conversations and insightful discussions; but you may also have a few heated debates and disagreements. So what should you—the leader—do in that situation? Here are some helpful tips on approaching conflict in your small group . . .

DEALING WITH CONFLICT

By Betty Veldman Wieland

Conflict is a normal part of small group life. In fact, if we don't have conflict, someone is not being honest. People are just too different from one another to avoid it completely. I do not like conflict. It makes me feel, well, conflicted! At the same time, I believe that understanding the nature of conflict and being prepared to deal with it as a small group leader, coach, or staff person is essential for people's spiritual growth and for a small group ministry to thrive.

The following guidelines have been helpful for me in dealing with conflict and may help you as well in your small group leadership role.

Know How You Deal with Conflict

The old adage "Physician, heal thyself!" truly applies here. Leaders who understand their own conflict management style approach conflict in an informed way. We all have strengths and weaknesses in dealing with conflict. Whether we will be helpful or a hindrance may depend on our understanding of what we bring to the conflict table. The Thomas-Kilmann Conflict Mode Inventory is a helpful tool for understanding the various conflict management styles. What is your primary style? Do you compete or collaborate? Do you compromise and accommodate or try to avoid conflict completely? No one style is right for every situation, but understanding your primary response will help to keep conflict in perspective.

I like to avoid conflict. When I confront it, I first look for a compromise. Knowing that about myself has been important when I need to die to my "preferred" conflict management style in order to do what is best for others. I remember well when I needed to confront a small group leader about talking too much. I tried tactfully, gently and indirectly to approach the subject. The leader looked me straight in the eye and asked, "Betty, what are you trying to say to me?" My astonishment at such a direct approach must have been written all over my face because the leader leaned forward, touched my arm and said, "Please, I need to hear this from you. Tell it to me straight."

Adapt to the Other Person

I learned a valuable lesson in the above situation. Though I wanted to avoid conflict, this leader needed me to be direct and confrontational. In dealing with conflict, we need to consider the conflict management style of those we deal with as well as our own style. We need to adapt to the people with whom we are dealing. This does not necessarily mean compromising—though it might—but it means communicating in a manner in which they can understand and relate.

Pray!

This may seem like a no-brainer, but it needs to be underscored. The potential for conflict to be destructive is huge. It is hard to be objective as a leader. We all have biases and personal viewpoints. There is great temptation to defer to our preferred outcome rather than to facilitate an honest confrontation of an issue. It takes being submissive to the Holy Spirit's leading to keep us honest and in tune with what God desires.

Think Gray and Listen

Discerning where God is leading in times of conflict includes reserving judgment until we have all the evidence. It is what *The Contrarian's*

Guide to Leadership calls to "think gray." Most issues are not black and white. We need to listen carefully—for feelings as well as facts—and to reserve judgment until all parties involved have had a fair hearing. Doing this builds trust. It also gives us the time needed to sense where the Holy Spirit is at work.

Differentiate Between Problems and People, Issues and Emotions, Facts and Feelings

The statement, "A problem well-defined is a problem half-solved" is especially true when dealing with conflict. When the focus is on the problem, whether a difference of opinion or perspective, the parties involved can together often reach a compromise or collaborate to come to a better outcome than each would have come to alone. We simply mediate and ask questions to clarify the issue. In such a case, the conflict is substantive and can be positive. It becomes an opportunity for growth and change.

Sometimes, however, the conflict is due to a personality conflict, and emotions run too deep to come to a positive outcome. When people begin attacking people instead of problems, the conflict is affective and, if left unchecked, can be highly destructive.

One of the most difficult things I have ever had to do is remove a volunteer leader from leadership. I did not do so lightly, but it became apparent that the leader in question was using a top-down, authoritative approach to intimidate people into doing what the leader wanted. Those who did not comply were personally undermined, belittled, and discredited. Everyone in the small group was up in arms. When I confronted the leader, I was personally attacked as well.

Be Willing to Take a Stand

When the above happened, I was tempted to apologize and back down. After all, avoidance is my primary conflict management style. However, this was not about me and it was not about the leader in question. It was about the issue at hand and the people affected by the conflict. The leader had supporters who were waiting to see how I would handle what had become a major problem. I needed to carefully and positively address the impasse at hand, to isolate the problem, and to address it without attacking any of the people involved.

Then, I needed to take responsibility for the decision I made. I called a special meeting of all the people involved to explain my decision. The leader chose not to attend. I remember well that a highly-respected member of the group and an advocate for the leader I had removed came and talked with me after the meeting. She admitted she was "loaded for bear" and ready to let me have it for the decision I made. Instead, she thanked me and said, "I have even more respect for you as a leader because of how you handled this situation." No one needed to know the nitty-gritty details of the conflict, but everyone needed to know it was handled prayerfully and with integrity, addressing the problem without attacking any person involved in the conflict. We can only do that on our knees.

Look for a Win-Win Solution

I looked desperately for a win-win solution in this situation but found none because the leader in question could not get beyond blaming others and attacking them personally. In conflict, a win-win is always the solution of choice. It safeguards the dignity of the people involved, respects the diversity that God created, and allows for a difference in perspectives. Isolating what we can compromise on helps us to be able to hold our ground on those things that are non-negotiable. A win-win requires that both parties seek the good of the other, not just their own. One cannot dig in one's heels and declare, "I'm right and you need to come over to where I am." When that happens, someone loses. Though there may be principles we cannot compromise, there are usually extraneous circumstances that we can. When we can collaborate to come to an even better outcome, that is the best win-win of all.

Leave the Results to God

In the end, we do our best in dealing with conflict and leave the results to God. Not everyone will like us when we mediate conflict. That is the price of leadership. The leader I removed from leadership has never spoken to me again. That is painful for me, but I followed the above steps and did as I believe God directed me. Though the leader may continue to blame me, I have peace in knowing that the group involved benefited from my willingness to make that hard decision. The group itself thrived under new leadership. Being faithful and obedient to God's call in leadership is the most important part of dealing with conflict. That is what God honors most.

Betty Veldman Wieland; copyright 2005 by Christianity Today International. Originally appeared on www.SmallGroups.com.

■ Notes

1. Krista Tippett, "The New Evangelical Leaders, Part 1: Jim Wallis," Speaking of Faith, http://speakingoffaith.publicradio.org/programs/ jimwallis/transcript.shtml.

■ Notes

■ Notes

■ Notes

■ Notes

■ Notes